Boyhood to Manhood

Rochelle Brock and Richard Greggory Johnson III
Executive Editors

Vol. 65

The Black Studies and Critical Thinking series
is part of the Peter Lang Education list.
Every volume is peer reviewed and meets
the highest quality standards for content and production.

PETER LANG
New York • Bern • Frankfurt • Berlin
Brussels • Vienna • Oxford • Warsaw

Boyhood to Manhood

Deconstructing Black Masculinity through a Life Span Continuum

Edited by C. Spencer Platt,
Darryl B. Holloman
& Lemuel W. Watson

PETER LANG
New York • Bern • Frankfurt • Berlin
Brussels • Vienna • Oxford • Warsaw

Library of Congress Cataloging-in-Publication Data

From boyhood to manhood: deconstructing Black masculinity through a life
span continuum / edited by C. Spencer Platt, Darryl B. Holloman, Lemuel W. Watson.
pages cm. — (Black studies and critical thinking; v. 65)
Includes bibliographical references.
1. African American men—Education (Higher) 2. African American men—
Social conditions. 3. African American men—Race identity. 4. Masculinity.
5. African American male college students. 6. Academic achievement—United States.
I. Platt, C. Spencer.
LC2781.F75   378.1'982996073—dc23   2014038331
ISBN 978-1-4331-2560-7 (hardcover)
ISBN 978-1-4331-2559-1 (paperback)
ISBN 978-1-4539-1445-8 (e-book)
ISSN 1947-5985

Bibliographic information published by **Die Deutsche Nationalbibliothek**.
Die Deutsche Nationalbibliothek lists this publication in the "Deutsche
Nationalbibliografie"; detailed bibliographic data are available
on the Internet at http://dnb.d-nb.de/.

© 2015 Peter Lang Publishing, Inc., New York
29 Broadway, 18th floor, New York, NY 10006
www.peterlang.com

All rights reserved.
Reprint or reproduction, even partially, in all forms such as microfilm,
xerography, microfiche, microcard, and offset strictly prohibited.

Table of Contents

List of Figures..vii

Foreword.. ix
    C. P. Gause

Acknowledgments xiii

Introduction 1
    Spencer Platt, Darryl B. Holloman, and Lemuel W. Watson

Chapter One: First-Year Experience: Engaging and Supporting
    Millennial Black Males During the First Year of College 5
    Patrick E. Turner

Chapter Two: Am I Not a Man and a Brother? I Am a Man...................... 21
    LaGarrett King

Chapter Three: All Eyes on Me: High-Profile African American Male
    Student-Athletes' Social Transition into Predominantly White
    Institutions of Higher Education 43
    Darren D. Kelly

Chapter Four: Brothers Gonna Work It Out: Black Male Academics
  Negotiating Mentorship, Fatherhood, and Partnerhood
  in a Community Context 69
  Richard J. Reddick and James Thomas

Chapter Five: The State of Health Among Black Men in the
  United States: Implications of Demographic Heterogeneity................ 83
  Juanita J. Chinn and Andrea K. Henderson

Chapter Six: Everyday Struggle: Critical Race Theory and
  Black Male Doctoral Student Experience................................. 107
  C. Spencer Platt

Chapter Seven: Pimp or Pauper: An Autoethnography of Black
  Gangstaism's Prevalence with College-Going Black
  Males at One Historically White Institution 131
  Stanley Ellis

Contributors... 153

List of Figures

"Am I Not a Man and a Brother?" Courtesy of the Library of Congress............ 22
Negro Life in Georgia. Photo Album, vol. 4, ca. 1900. Print and Photographs Division. Library of Congress. Bequest of Daniel A. P. Murray, ca. 1926 (42.7) Digital ID# ppmsca-08762................................. 31
Paul Robeson as Othello.. 33
Major Charles Young with officers in Mexico. Source: US Cavalry, NPS; public domain..................................... 34
Ms. Juanita E. Jackson visiting the Scottsboro Boys, January 1937. Library of Congress Prints and Photographs Division. Visual Materials from the NAACP records (reproduction number LC-USZ62-123456).............. 36
Emmett Till and his mother, Mamie Bradley, ca. 1955. Gelatin Silver Print. Visual Materials from the NAACP Records, Prints and Photographs Division, Library of Congress (7). Courtesy of the NAACP. Digital ID: cph 3f06304... 36
Rodney King and L.A. police. CNN via Getty Images........................... 37

Foreword

C. P. GAUSE

Scholars, researchers, and policymakers continue to inform our communities that children of color, particularly "Black males," lag behind every other demographic in academic achievement and success. The current representation—or even construction, if you will allow—of Black males in popular culture and social media often conflicts with the prevailing notions that have traditionally surrounded the ideology of masculine power and identity, particularly as that identity is juxtaposed against the idea of White male masculinity.

The heavily policed and illuminated image of the black male is the object of adolescent intrigue, public sphere fascination, and global product placement and consumption via commodification. Many scholars and policymakers continue to limit the analyses of black masculinity to detached statistical data and reports devoid of the authentic (re) presentations of the voice and performance of black masculinities across multiple spheres. Dr. Spencer Platt, Dr. Darryl B. Holloman, and Dr. Lemuel W. Watson, however, as editors of this volume, *From Boyhood to Manhood: Deconstructing Black Masculinity through a Life Span Continuum*, bring together a fantastic team of authors and researchers who move from the realm of objectifying the black male and reifying false deficit statistical constructions to investigating and interrogating the multi-dimensional complexities of being a black man in America. I am quite impressed with this volume and applaud the authors for utilizing qualitative, mixed methods, quantitative, case studies and various sampling methodologies and theoretical frameworks as tools to deconstruct black masculinity through the life span of today's black male.

Given the power of social media, the global community is witness to a wide variety of mediated imagery. However, the representation of the Black male is almost exclusively the duffle bag boy—drug runner, money carrier, thug. He is depicted as an aggressive, no-holds-barred bad boy, often a lifelong convict, always in and out of jail. The basis for this myopic representation—particularly in a perceived post-racial America—is rooted within the misconstrued "maleness" and power associated with crime. Particularly, as the criminal lifestyle has been glorified for Black males through music, language, fashion, and behavioral norms. The underlying messages in these images of Black masculinity are ones of heteronormativity, homophobia, and patriarchy. This volume deconstructs this popularized caricature of Black masculinity and offers insight into the varied and nuanced performances and experiences of Black masculinity. I believe Black males across the globe are one of the most powerful creations ever known to humanity and this volume serves as a testament to this belief. This volume interrogates the intersections of race, class, and gender with regard to Black masculinity and it moves the discourse across multiple epistemological landscapes.

As I reflect on the title, *From Boyhood to Manhood: Deconstructing Black Masculinity Through a Life Span Continuum*, I am reminded of a very important fact in our culture. The stigmatization of Black males has been embraced not only by America at large, but most sadly by the African American community as well. The dominant culture continues to perpetuate negative imagery of African American males through mass media, much of which is performed, produced, and written by Black men and women. Most notably, this negative construction of Black masculinity is promoted by hip-hop artists, often supported by a multibillion-dollar music conglomerate. This persistent imagery further perpetuates the ongoing demise of the African American male. We know cultural norms are learned through experience of and exposure to modeled values and behaviors. The construction of values and culture, and of Black masculinity, are communicated to our youth through this pervasive imagery and we can see those behaviors and beliefs being adopted by the next generation. These patterns become inscribed adaptive culture mechanisms—they become their truth, their swag, and their being.

The political disturbances and cultural re-articulation of the Black male image requires new contextualization and different interpretive strategies. Black heterosexual masculinity is the basis of how society understands and relates to Black males: hero worship in the case of rappers; naturalization and commodification of bodies in the case of athletes; fear in the case of Black gang members; and respect as noble warriors in the case of Afrocentric nationalists and Fruit of Islam. Despite the variety of these figures, it is nevertheless the same Black body—super star athlete, indignant rapper, menacing gang member, ad model, appropriate middle-class professional, movie star—onto which competing and conflicting claims about (and for) Black masculinity are thrust. The mediated images of Black masculinity work symbolically in a number of directions at once; they challenge and disturb racial and class constructions of Blackness. They also rewrite and re-inscribe the patriarchal and heterosexual basis of masculine privilege (and domination) based on gender and sexuality. This book provides opportunities to disrupt these images and our understanding of Black masculinity, moving the discourse in a positive direction towards freeing society and Black males from the confines of these persistent cultural norms.

This volume furthers the discourse on Black masculinity in a variety of ways. The editors and authors create, actualize, and live out counter-narratives to these aforementioned mediated hegemonic constructions of the bestial, hypersexualized, aggressive, co-opted, and commodified Black male image and provide spaces for understanding, patience, and intimacy. In essence, the editors and authors seek out, produce, and construct knowledge that represents multilingual, multi-ethnic, and nonconforming gender identities and roles. In short, this work provides us with a sense of hope! Hope that things, although troubling, may not be as dire as they appear on the surface. Hope that things can and will change. Hope that the complexity of what it means to be Black and male should be further analyzed if adequate solutions are to be derived for those men who struggle against the confines of this construct. Hope on the eve of Maya Angelou's transition to a higher celestial realm that Black men too must still rise.

Acknowledgments

Spencer Platt
I would like to acknowledge and thank my family, friends, mentors and colleagues for theirs support. I would especially like to acknowledge the late Wanda Hendricks-Bellamy for believing in me.

Darryl Holloman
There are many to acknowledge but I would especially like to mention my beloved late brother David Jemel Holloman and the men who keep me going Glyn, Delbert and Delvin

Lemuel Watson
I would like to acknowledge my late father, Lem Watson, for his spirit and wisdom and my late brother-in-law, Tony L. Smith, for being a tremendous father—both men were pillars for our community.

Introduction

SPENCER PLATT, DARRYL B. HOLLOMAN,
AND LEMUEL W. WATSON

Black people have unique stories that beg to be told in numerous ways and from multiple perspectives. However, to date, an understanding of the Black experience within contemporary American society has largely been communicated by the visual imagery promulgated by popular media. These often fictionalized images are generally negative and disturbing, but what is more disturbing is how the depictions are internalized by some Black men and then used as the measure by which they view and define themselves. Consequently, the multidimensionality of the Black male experience must continuously be shared in order to provide a more accurate and positive representation of how Black men develop throughout the course of their lives.

The overarching goal of this book is to examine the multiple dimensions and perspectives regarding the roles that Black men occupy within our contemporary society. A secondary goal is to broaden how Black males view their own multiple identities. These diverse personal and professional identities impact the political, social, and economic climate in many ways in the United States. The book is meant to highlight a number of topics relevant to the experiences of Black males and to reflect on the diversity and depth of what it means to be American, international, Black, and male—in essence, a critical lifespan approach to how Black men perceive and relate to masculinity. Understanding Black men from such a holistic viewpoint is essential to the continued strength and vitality of Black social and family structures, as well as places of business and educational spheres, particularly in lieu of the challenges faced by Black people, especially Black men, in the 21st century.

The editors and fellow authors of this book believe that it is our responsibility to expand the dialogue on how best to analyze and interrogate the intersection of the multiple identities found among Black men. This may influence how helping professions tailor their approach when interpreting the challenges faced by Black men and in determining how to develop the most appropriate solutions for overcoming those challenges. When developing this book, we often discussed how important it was to present the Black male discourse in a different context than the deficit model that is commonly projected upon Black men. This does not mean that Black men do not face challenges, but it is important to acknowledge that most Black men, like most men generally, ultimately strive to be the best fathers, professionals, brothers, sons, academics, uncles, and grandfathers that they can possible become.

Identifying and understanding the complex and varied identities of contemporary Black men, the challenges these constructions pose to Black men and society, and what possible solutions might be offered to address these challenges requires a multidisciplinary approach and diverse lines of inquiry. While there is a rich and expansive body of scholarship discussing the nature, identity, and position of black women in society this work is attempting to expand a similar discussion taking place about Black males. Just as Black feminist scholarship has had feminism to frame their discourse, masculinity scholarship likewise informs the discourse on black masculinity. This book will likewise engage with the not insubstantial body of scholarship on masculinity generally. The experiences of Black men are often discussed not in terms of masculinity or social construction, but rather from more statistically driven and deficit-focused approaches about their health, fatherhood, professions, or, more tragically, their prison records, low graduation rates, and their deaths. The purpose of this book is to provide a venue for exploring the experiences of Black men, while realizing that we have only begun to scratch the surface of what it means to be a Black man within society today.

PURPOSE AND FOCUS

The purpose of this book is to bring a more open and honest discussion regarding the intersection of multiple identities found among Black males within contemporary society. Through these chapters, the reader will be able to reflect on the vast array of differences that exist among Black males, shedding light on the numerous and varied perceptions on race, health, (dis)ability, socioeconomic status, incarceration, boyhood, historical accounts, ethnicity, employment, religion, and sexuality. This book helps to broaden the current reductive understandings about collective and individual Black male identities. In doing so, it helps those who work with Black men to expand their understandings of this group in order to develop innovative ways of working with, counseling, mentoring, and educating them.

This book seeks to highlight specifically how Black men struggle with the demands of a culture guided by strict gendered norms. These norms often require men to conform to "masculine" behaviors. This rigid societal expectation may cause anxiety or fear of being ostracized if they fail to display what are deemed appropriate "male" behaviors. This influence on the development of men, particularly Black men, often dictates or limits the social, emotional, economic, and academic roles that they play within society. Subsequently, this impacts their overall interactions with the community, their families, and their partners. The ability for Black men to explore and embrace other possibilities of constructing their personal and professional realities, outside of the narrow construct of socially approved masculinity, creates new and promising opportunities for them within contemporary society.

The qualitative, quantitative, and historical data presented in this book provides a new understanding about the roles in society that Black men play. Specifically, the authors present research findings from several fields of study, encompassing a broad range of methodologies to include quantitative, qualitative, mixed methods, case studies, and various sampling techniques. The book is organized around several broad topical areas and is intended to fill gaps in our knowledge about how Black males engage across multiple kinds of institutions and how those experiences affect their development. Most importantly, this book brings to the forefront the voices of both well-known, seasoned academics as well as emerging scholars. This was done intentionally to provide a fresh approach that will resonate with a wide readership. Additionally, this diverse approach fosters innovative and creative ways to conduct research, and more importantly, to understand research questions. The range of experience presented in this book also provides inspiration for budding scholars that their voices, too, should be discovered and heard.

AUDIENCE

Race, class, socioeconomic status, sexual orientation, and gender continue to be social and political issues that affect all facets of life in the U.S. This book was written to be used by educators, administrators, policymakers, social service agencies, church leaders, and others who are concerned with the experiences of Black men in various settings. Those who teach in African American or gender studies programs will also find this book useful in their classes and in developing their research agendas. This book will serve as a reader for those in the social and economic professions—we consider to be those professions and fields that are interested in individuals who are in need of developing their "authentic" sense of self. Instructors of undergraduate and graduate courses in teacher education, social foundations, student affairs, policy studies, counseling, health, and similar areas will also find this book useful and insightful. Finally, the book is written so that the purpose of each chapter is easily understood and the book avoids overly technical language when providing analysis and results. The editors make every attempt to present language that is accessible to various reading audiences.

There are a number of books in circulation today that focus on Black professionals. These books tend to be highly specialized and geared toward specific fields of interest, and they rarely address issues related to both Black men who are within and outside of the academy. What is unique about this book is that it is designed to present a collection of research findings and best practices from several disciplines and fields of study with a focus on the totality of the Black male experience throughout his lifespan. This volume will express the views of individuals who work with boys and teens, as well as record the experiences of middle-aged and older men. The book will explore men who thrive in professional settings, as well as those who deal with social issues and whose lives may fall outside of acceptable social norms. In providing this expansive view of the Black male experience, this book opens new ground by providing empirical evidence which both validates prior research, while also offering cutting-edge work on how Black men prepare to enter, facilitate, and integrate within contemporary social and political structures.

CHAPTER ONE

First-Year Experience: Engaging and Supporting Millennial Black Males During the First Year of College

PATRICK E. TURNER

A persisting challenge facing many postsecondary institutions in the United States is the retention of Millennial Black males during their first year of college. Millennials are categorized as those individuals born between the years of 1982 and 2002 (Rickes, 2009). In 2003–2004, 16% of freshman students that enrolled in a U.S. postsecondary education institution in 2003 left the institution without completing a degree or certificate by 2004 (Ross et al., 2012). Black males accounted for a quarter of that percentage. Additionally, less than a third of freshman Black males enrolled in a four-year college will graduate with a degree within six years (Schmidt, 2008). Though Black males enter postsecondary institutions with higher aspirations and initial engagement, when compared to other races and ethnic groups, this population of students is less likely to academically persist or reach their goals (Mangan, 2014). Unfortunately, Black males lose that initial excitement about the educational experience and eventually become unmotivated, disengaged, and discouraged (Mangan, 2014). The motivation or lack thereof to persist academically directly impacts retention, degree obtainment, future career opportunities, income earning potential, and marketability (Palmer & Young, 2009).

Since the 1980s, research data has indicated a marginal increase in the college enrollment of Millennial Black males but the data can be misleading without a broader and expansive understanding (Frierson, Pearson, & Wyche, 2009; Palmer, 2009). There is reason to applaud the slight increase in college enrollment, yet Black males are still disproportionately underachieving in all academic measures when compared to Whites and other minority groups (Bush & Bush, 2010; Palmer & Young, 2009). The retention and degree completion rates for Millennial Black males are starkly lower than that of other racial and ethnic groups (Palmer & Young, 2009).

An exhaustive amount of quantitative studies have been conducted that examine the relationship between African American male and college, but there exist scant or limited qualitative research that gives voice to Millennial Black males and their first-year college experience. According to Davis (1995), the voices of Black males are often dismissed or misunderstood. This is unfortunate because their perspectives and personal narratives could possibly lead to the construction of solutions that could unravel this complex issue. What institutional factors, programs, or characteristics hinder or create a meaningful first-year experience for Millennial Black males and how do we know? Data reports derived from quantitative assessments and mechanisms offer a limited perspective that does not paint a complete picture of the first-year experience, in addition to excluding the human component. Qualitative research is important to understanding the complexities surrounding the retention and attrition of Black males in college. Comprehending human actions and behaviors often requires this information to be conveyed in a descriptive and verbatim format that can be done through narrative data techniques such as interviews and self-description (Sieyes, 2008).

The focus of this chapter will be on those institutional factors that serve as obstacles or supports to the transition of Millennial Black males into the social and academic environment during their first year of college. Further, practices and changes institutions can implement to ensure a seamless and engaging first-year experience will be discussed. Seven African American males who attended a large four-year research institution were interviewed to collect their candid opinions, feedback, and perspectives regarding their first-year experience. All students were of traditional college age (18–22) and classified as a freshman or sophomore. The data were extracted from a larger qualitative research study consisting of 30 participants that explored Millennial first-year college experience. The topic is relevant and vital to conducting meaningful conversation and discussion about the reevaluation of the quality of postsecondary education in the U.S., Black male student integration, student engagement, social justice, building human and social capital, and constructing strategies that increase the retention and graduation rate of Millennial Black males.

DETERIORATING PIPELINE

Over the last 30 years, a focal point for postsecondary institutions in the United States has been student retention and the first-year experience; even so, higher education still struggles to construct programs and services that retain a large portion of its students (Simmons, 2013). According to Simmons (2013), students prematurely leave colleges and universities without the institution possessing a clear understanding of the reasons, contributing factors, and influences of their departure. A significant portion of these students leave within the first year of college, which is not only problematic for those individuals, but also to the institution and society at large. According to the American College and Testing Program (ACT), in 2007–2008 the national average of freshman students returning to the same institution for their sophomore year was 66%, compared to 68% in 2006–2007 (Burshong, 2009). Though some postsecondary institutions are experiencing some gain in freshmen retention, nationally there is a steady decline in freshman students returning for their sophomore or second year, especially among African American males.

African American males possess the lowest first-year college retention rate as well as overall college performance when compared to other racial and ethnic groups (Simmons, 2013; Frierson et al., 2009). The National Center for Education Statistics (Ross et al., 2012) reported that 22% of freshman Black males enrolled in a postsecondary institution in 2003–2004 dropped out by 2004. According to Schmidt (2008), less than one-third of Black males attending a four-year postsecondary institution will graduate in six years with a bachelor degree. Unfortunately, an increasing number of males drop out within the first year without completing a degree or certificate program (Ross et al., 2012).

Frierson, Pearson, and Wyche (2009) referred to this occurrence as a "leakage" or deterioration of the education and academic pipeline of Black males. Unfortunately, the leak begins during the early years—around the third grade. Researchers argue this is the stage when young Black boys start experiencing an identity crisis associated with masculinity, lack of family resources and discrimination (Polite & Davis, 1999). Polite and Davis (1999) stated Black boys' reaction to the crisis is usually displayed through anger, frustration, and aggressive behavior because of poor coping skills. Teachers are challenged with how to effectively manage this behavior in addition to constructing effective teaching strategies that address the learning needs and cultural experiences of young Black boys. Palmer and Young (2009) argued that during the developmental stages of elementary and secondary education, instead of engaging Black males, some teachers and counselors often discourage Black males from attending college. This behavior on the part of educators further perpetuates and reinforces the stereotype that Black males are uneducated, dysfunctional and lack the intellectual capacity to learn or be taught. The educational pipeline is allowed to continue to decay and erode, thus weakening the connectivity and support for Black males. The achievement gap between Black males and other ethnic and gender groups widens as Black boys become academically disengaged, assigned to special education classes, or characterized as dysfunctional, criminals, or hypersexual. As a result, Black males perform at a disproportionately lower academic rate and face more expulsions and other disciplinary actions in school than any other ethnic groups and gender (Polite & Davis, 1999; Palmer & Young, 2009).

Over time the factors contributing to the deteriorating pipeline have become so complex and massive that the problem requires a massive solution or solutions just as complex to address the interconnected parts. Such solutions come not only at a high price, but also require an extreme overhaul of the entire educational system at all levels. The deterioration of the pipeline resembles the progression of an illness left untreated. Researchers believe the damage has becomes so severe and far-reaching that educators, leaders and policymakers disagree on how or where to begin and what solution would work best (Frierson et al., 2009). Institutions are embarrassed or even reluctant to discuss the issue for fear of further stigmatizing Black males generally or admitting the lack of attention that higher education has paid to the struggles of Black males (Schmidt, 2008). Subsequently, Black males are slipping through the gaping holes of a deteriorating educational pipeline at an alarming rate.

Scholars have provided many possible reasons and developed various schools of thought on the deterioration of the pipeline and the contributing factors to the low retention rate of Black males in college. A common idea is that institutional environment and social factors play a major role in student engagement and identity development (Frierson et al., 2009; Dancy, 2011). Student engagement and identity development are critical topics when not only attempting to define the relationship between Black males and college, but also in placing those relationships in context. One commonly surmised reason for the low academic performance among Black males is that they do not view high academic achievement and educational success as relevant to their experience and plight (Polite & Davis, 1999). In fact, studious behavior (e.g., studying and good grades) is often viewed as a feminine trait and less socially attractive, so therefore counterproductive to the masculine male image (Polite & Davis, 1999). Additionally, acceptance and adoption of these successful academic behaviors would bring into question the student's "Blackness" or commitment to their cultural identity. Students consciously or unconsciously develop destructive attitudes and behaviors toward education such as not speaking standard English and not striving for academic excellence and achievement for fear of being perceived as acting "White" (Frierson et al., 2009; Signithia & Ogbu, 1986).

Throughout the educational pipeline Black males must navigate what Frierson, Pearson, and Wyche (2009) refer to as the "three warring souls." The three warring souls, which are in constant battle, are a Black man in Black culture, a Black man in White culture, and a gifted Black male. Simultaneously, Black males struggle when making social, political, and educational decisions that often bring into conflict the two realities of an African American male living within a Euro-American culture—the reality that identifies with African American culture and values, and the reality of Euro-American culture and values. Attempting to find balance between these two conflicting realities can cause anger and indignation because rejecting either could result in alienation and the loss of economic opportunities and personal growth (Polite & Davis, 1999). Polite and Davis (1999) state,

> If the individual identifies solely with the Eurocentric values of individualism, competitiveness, emotion suppression, power and dominance, he or she, may achieve success at the cost of being isolated from the African American community. Conversely, if the individual identifies solely with African American values, he or she may not develop many of the necessary skills to survive in the occupational mainstream. (p. 70)

The conflicting realities and identity crisis can make the recruitment and retention of Black males in higher education challenging for colleges and universities.

The deterioration of the educational pipeline for Black males has become so urgent and vast that action on every level of education is required. Educational leaders, scholars, policymakers, and researchers must form a collaborative effort to construct and develop institutional policies, instructional practices, and programs that effectively engage Black males socially and academically, especially during the first year of college. Schmidt (2008) writes, "the biggest challenge in better serving minority college students is not creating new knowledge about how to help them; it is creating new incentives for institutional leaders to act on the knowledge that already exists" (p. 6).

A NEW GENERATION OF LEARNERS

A new generation of learners has arrived on college and university campuses that challenges the traditional ways institutions of higher education provide services and support. The generation is referred to as Millennials or Generation Y. Strauss and Howe (2003) categorized the group as those individuals born between the years of 1982 and 2002. Although persons within the cohort possess individual traits, generationally common values and behaviors have been identified. Millennials are considered the largest generation since the Baby Boomers, culturally diverse, and possessing unique characteristics and traits that will transform society and force postsecondary institutions to rethink how services are designed and success measured (Strauss & Howe, 2003; Rickes, 2009; Torisk, 2011; Lowery, 2004). Lowery (2004) asserts that Millennials are a "new breed" of students with the extraordinary potential to change the landscape of U.S. college campuses, as well as society, in a profound way (p. 87).

Though each generation possesses distinguishable characteristics due to a shared experience of historical and social events, Millennials' share traits that are vastly different from those students that attended college 20 or 30 years ago. According to Monaco and Martin (2007), Millennials' collective behavioral pattern, personality traits, educational expectations, and mental processes are not only unique to the present educational atmosphere, but can also provide insight into a new-age orientation to teaching and learning. Millennials are viewed as having a "lack of professional boundaries influenced by socialization, a need to have immediate feedback, a sense of entitlement, a lack of critical thinking skills, unrealistic expectations, high level of parental involvement, and an expected 'how to guide' to succeed in and out of the classroom" (Monaco & Martin, 2007, p. 42). Students require more guidance and supervision than past generations and learn best in a collaborative, experiential, and structured environment. According to Tucker (2006), to create a meaningful learning experience, college and universities will be required to create a collaborative atmosphere that not only motivates Millennials to be self-reflective, but also promote active participation in constructing knowledge.

Strauss and Howe (2003) identified several core characteristics and traits associated with the Millennial generation: sheltered, team-players, conventional behavior, confident attitude, achievers, special, and pressured. Characteristics may manifest through behavioral patterns and actions. For example, Millennials sometimes possess an unrealistic or impractical confidence about their academic abilities, leaving students unaware of their unpreparedness or underpreparedness for the college environment (Lowery, 2004). A student may refuse to take remedial courses or seek out academic advisement and support when needed. Though academic resources and support are available, many students do not take advantage of these services, especially males. Male students are least likely to seek out support or request assistance when academic challenges are encountered (Schmidt, 2008).

THE FIRST-YEAR EXPERIENCE

The first year of college is critical to the academic success, social integration, retention, and persistence of students in the institutional environment. This is the time a freshman is making the transition from high school into the college environment, which can often be an uncomfortable and challenging experience. Some students will make a seamless and successful transition without many challenges while others may find the adjustment daunting and overwhelming. The enrollment of Black males in a four-year U.S. college or university accounted for less than 5% of all college enrolled students (Palmer & Young, 2009). On average, 25% of Black males dropped out or left the college or university within the first year without completing a degree or certificate. This level of attrition not only possesses challenges for that individual, but also has an adverse impact on Americans' educational, political, and economic system. Without a postsecondary degree, Black males are unable to obtain highly skilled jobs and society cannot capitalize on the intellectual talents and capital that could have been provided by that individual (Palmer & Young, 2009). The ability of the U.S. to compete in a global marketplace depends on having an educated populace. Understanding the complexities surrounding the retention of Black males requires identifying and isolating those influences that directly contribute or hinder the first-year experience.

In addition to formulating ideas about possible academic courses, majors, and career paths the first year is also a time for self-exploration. This period is when students start assessing their strengths and weaknesses, forming their social and cultural identities, and figuring out how those identities fit within the broader community. Now that the student has arrived on campus, what instructional strategies, programs, and services will be effective in maintaining this attention and interest?

Student engagement is an essential component to the social and academic integration of students into the academic environment. Whether a student persists academically or decides to leave an institution is directly influenced by the level of engagement or type of relationship that is formed by the institution. A less engaged student is more likely to leave an institution when facing academic challenges than a student that is actively involved in campus programs and events. Tinto (2006) argued that how well an institution establishes a relationship and nurtures that connection is not only vital to the lived experience of a student, but also college persistence. This act of engagement must be sustained past orientation and continue throughout matriculation. Access to higher education has become readily available for students, but many still fail to persist past the first year of college, especially underrepresented groups such as racial minorities (Seidman, 2012). What has been problematic is that postsecondary institutions are enrolling minority students, but are unable to retain the students through graduation. Colleges and universities invest large sums of money in programs, consultants, and interventions to meet the needs of these minority populations with little result. Seidman (2012) states,

> In spite of these additional programs and services, neither retention from first to second year nor graduation rates have improved over time. Logic dictates that the addition of programs and services should help improve their retention of students but this seems to not be the case. (p. 4)

New, creative, and innovative approaches need to be explored to construct interventions and programs that address the needs of this population of students. Increased knowledge of cultural backgrounds, experiences, and behaviors would aid in the design, implementation, and assessment of programmatic intervention.

Identity development refers to exploration and forming of one's core values, beliefs, characteristics, personality, gender, and behavior (Scott, Havice, Livingston, & Cawthon, 2012). Development is also inclusive of religion, ethnicity, sexual identity, racial/ethnic identity, and other individual traits that make up an individual. The process of identity development begins from birth and continues into adulthood. External factors such living environment, social surroundings, friends, and family shape how we view the world, others, and ourselves. The foundational structure starts forming when a parent provides the child with what is considered a gender-appropriate toy, teaching rituals, customs, family values, and traditions. This practice has long been a part of American culture. The Puritans believed in the "holy triad," which supported the belief that the development of a child rests with the parents, church, and school. Education and schooling have always played a critical role in identity development, gender roles, and social responsibility. Colleges and universities are considered places where students continue to explore their identity, challenge social norms, and learn how to negotiate multiple identities (Dancy, 2011).

For many males, especially Black males, making the psychological transition from boyhood to young adulthood can be a complex and intimidating process, especially when there is constant characterization of Black males as being thugs, hypermasculine, criminals, wayward fathers, and uneducated. Mangan (2013) believes that "ways in which Black and Latino male teens, especially those who reside in America's largest cities, [are] persistently portrayed in media and elsewhere negatively affect society's expectations of them and, at times, their expectations of themselves" (p. A9). The agency, culture, experiences, problems, and needs of Black males must be understood by college administrators in order to offer meaningful experiences that deconstruct negative stereotypes and provide a healthy environment for identify development and self-exploration.

METHODOLOGY

Purpose of the Study

The purpose of this qualitative case study is to explore and understand the supports and challenges Millennial African American males face during their first year of college when transitioning into the institutional environment. The subgroup of seven African American males was extracted from a larger research study consisting of 30 participants. Often the voices of African American males are ignored, disregarded, or misunderstood instead of used as tools in constructing effective college experiences. The qualitative research approach allowed the students to provide personal narratives and place their college experiences in context (Hilton, Wood, & Lewis, 2012). The intention and hope of the qualitative study is to provide a platform for their voices to be heard and contribute to what is sometimes an uncomfortable conversation about African American male experiences in the educational system.

The seven African American males consisted of five sophomores and two freshman between the ages of 18 and 22 from a variety of academic majors. Each participant was asked 23 semi-structured interview questions regarding the subject covering the topics of overall college experience, freshman services, obstacles, and supports. All interviews were conducted face-to-face and on average lasted 45 minutes. The men were asked to be as honest as possible and reassured that all names would remain confidential and no identifiable information would be used. Participants were informed that an audio recording device would be used only if their approval was granted. If approval was not granted handwritten notes would be taken to document interview. The participants were willing to have their voices recorded and were eager to know that their experiences would be documented and valued.

Research Questions

The objective of the overall and broader scope of the qualitative research was answering the central question, "How do the participants describe and reflect on their first-year college experience?" The overarching research question was segmented into three subquestions (SQ) that addressed specific aspects critical to the first-year college experience:

- SQ1: What perceived activities and programs engage freshman college students into the first-year college environment?
- SQ2: What perceived obstacles do college freshman experience in transitioning into the first year of college?
- SQ3: What perceived activities and programs might enhance the transition into the college environment for freshman students?

Institution

The men selected for this research study attended a larger public research institution located in the southern United States. The institution is located in an urban downtown city area with an enrollment of 33,000 students that represent over

150 countries. Undergraduate and graduate programs are offered in a variety of disciplines and academic majors. This particular site was selected because the institution has made intentional efforts to implement first-year programs and initiatives for African American males to assist in successful transition into the college environment.

Participant Profile

Seven African American male students enrolled in a four-year university were selected to participate in the study. Participants consisted of two freshman students who were enrolled in the fall of the 2010–2011 school year and five sophomores who were in attendance in 2011–2012. Respondents were of traditional college age (18–22) with a median age of 19. Participants were classified as full-time students and academic majors consisted of a variety disciplines (see Table 1).

Table 1: African American Male Participant Demographic Information.

Number of Participants	Median Age	Grade Level	Major(s)	Financial Assistance
2	18	Freshman	Finance and Accounting	Scholarships
5	20	Sophomore	Journalism, Finance, Marketing, Political Science, and Business Economics	Scholarships, Loans, and Grants

Freshman participants were 18 years of age and considered full-time students, taking a minimum of 12 academic course hours. Tuitions and academic fees were paid by either merit-based funding or grants and neither student was employed. Both students lived on campus and declared majors were Finance and Accounting. Their parents' educational level ranged from 12th grade to some college courses with three of the four parents having taken some postsecondary college courses. This is in line with the fact that many Millennial generation students tend to have one or more parents or guardians who have some form of postsecondary education. Their parents could possibly offer some insight or advice into navigating the college environment.

The sophomore participants ages ranged from 19 to 21 with a median age of 19 years. All of the participants lived on campus with two working part-time to cover tuition and fees. A combination of merit-based scholarships, grants, and loans were needed to cover academic expenses. Academic majors spanned a variety of disciplines, such as of marketing, journalism, political science, business economics, and finance. Their parents' educational level ranged from the 11th grade to doctoral degree.

The average GPA for the seven male participants was 3.0 on a 4.0 scale.

THE FINDINGS

The finding of the study revealed that the factors that most enable or challenge the first-year transition of Millennial African American males into the college environment revolved around three major themes: social engagement, instructor-student relationship, and study skills and behavior.

Social Engagement

The social engagement of the freshman males was not only critical to decreasing the nervousness associated with having to adjust to an unfamiliar environment, but also to identity development. Unfortunately, though the seven males possess high GPAs ranging from 3.0–4.11, each of the men entered the institution without any real academic expectation or goals. Of the seven participants, only one had received academic or career guidance from an advisor, teacher, or counselor.

All the participants had a list of social expectations and plans. The social component of the college experience was extremely important to them; many attended the institution because of its culturally diverse population, networking opportunities, and urban, downtown location. The participants believed that campus activities such as the parties, freshman week, Greek life, and sporting events fostered a sense of belonging and helped students determine where they fit within the campus community. This mental ease is referred to by Roberts and Styron (2009) as a "psychological comfort." Involvement in intramural sports, co-curricular activities, African American male fraternities, social clubs, and professional organization was helpful in building self-confidence, creating a sense of belonging and navigating the identity as both a male and Black. Terrion and Daoust (2011–2012) state that prior academic behavior may influence academic performance, but campus social atmosphere determines whether or not a student stays or leaves after the first year. Participant SM5 provides some advice to new incoming freshmen:

> Soon as they come in, I would say join an organization. That would be the very first step, is like join an organization where it's gonna force you to, to be around the people that you need to be around, whether it's, you know, an academic organization or a social fraternity or something, so like you already get those personal connections and networks...so that,

you know, you're automatically hearing about what's going on campus, what's going on off campus, what classes you take, what can you do with this degree, so that, that does a, that's a very big help because these people are, either they went through the same circumstances that you went through, or they're going through them with you while you're going through them. So you definitely need to be around those people. Another thing would just be, just have fun with it.

Participants believed that a student is at a disadvantage when there is little participation or active involvement in campus activities and events. Social engagement was considered one of several components of the college experience which was viewed as critical to academic persistence. This can be heard in participant SM6's following statement:

> First thing I would say was get involved because—because if you just come to school and you just leave, you know, you're, you're missing out on not only like, you're not only like putting yourself at a disadvantage because there's like a lot of information and stuff you're missing out from other people and other experiences, but you're just like, you're just missing the college experience and I feel like that's what a lot of freshmen do and maybe that's why a lot of, a lot of them fall out because they don't feel connected to [the college] at all.

Instructor-Student Relationship

The instructor-student relationship was an important factor to student success and academic achievement identified by the participants. Fostering an interactive and collaborative instructor-student relationship affected the level of engagement, classroom participation, and comprehension of classroom material. The participants were less likely to ask questions, seek assistance when facing academic challenges, or participate in classroom discussions if the instructor was perceived as unapproachable or unfriendly. All the participants believed that establishing a positive and healthy instructor-student relationship was necessary to academic achievement and success. Three of the seven participants felt comfortable discussing academic issues with their instructors and were able to foster an interactive relationship. The results were an increased enthusiasm and excitement about the course and institution, and a sense of pride and commitment to academic achievement. Frierson, Pearson, and Wyche (2009) found that African American males feel more empowered and motivated when their instructors have high expectations or display interest in their academic careers. The other five participants referred to their relationships with their instructors as disconnected, intimidating, not helpful, sterile, and not special. Interaction with their instructors mainly occurred through email exchanges rather than the participant-preferred face-to-face. Of note, all of the participants expected to not be acknowledged by or to develop an interactive and collaborative relationship with their instructors. SM2 stated,

> I knew that you couldn't really connect with every single professor. There are some professors that you won't even get to know their name or they won't know you personally. So I had to make an effort to meet my professors that, so that I could get extra help or I could get, or inside on things, so I knew that would be a challenge for me as well as any other freshman student, meeting professors in large classrooms.

One male student emphasized that instructors need to be more understanding of the African American male experience and make a conscious effort to connect with students in addition to providing assistance. Several factors were mentioned that influence the instructor-student relationship: instructor helpfulness, individual attention, one-on-one meetings, instructor accessibility, and the instructor's knowledge of each student. Participants also encouraged students to take the initiative in developing meaningful relationships with their instructors in order to have a successful academic career. SM8 stated,

> Talk to your professors. Have a relationship with your professors. No matter how big the class is, even if it's a lecture class, sit in the front of the class. My first instructor, well, one that stands out, was my English instructor and I liked her so much I ended up taking her again the very next semester for the second part of English.

Study Skills and Behaviors

A major challenge encountered by 80% of the participants was not having the necessary study skills and behavioral practices to ensure academic success. Many of the participants entered college either unprepared or underprepared for the academic environment. Participant FM6 stated, "Learning how to study…in high school I really didn't study like that, so now I am trying to increase my studying. The school should help us get good study habits." Terrion and Daoust (2011–2012) maintain, "For many students the first year at a university, simply establishing a systematic approach to studying (both keeping up with readings and homework, preparing for tests and exams) in the university is a challenge" (p. 321). Often, the participants internalized these challenges and temporarily lost confidence in their abilities. Frierson, Pearson, and Wyche (2009) viewed this as a consequence of stereotypical threats, which sometimes paralyze Black male students with the fear that the negative assumptions about their academic abilities might be true. Participants experienced a feeling of isolation when left to their own devices. The participants were not accustomed to quizzes and exams covering five to six chapters or being responsible for material that may or may not have been mentioned in the instructors lecture. In the words of participant SM5:

> I learned like real quickly that I can't, I couldn't just like sit there like I did in high school and just kinda, I'd just skate by just by like going home, looking at PowerPoints on the Internet and just trying to take the test like that because in a lot of my classes, some of

the PowerPoints don't have all the information, you know? Like if you're just reading the PowerPoints and you're not taking the chance to look at the book and not going through the book like weeks in advance, you're, you're missing like tons of information. High school studying techniques included the memorization and regurgitation of the instructor's notes so no systematic strategy for outlining and reading chapters had been developed.

Fortunately, the participants were able to solicit assistance from peers, academic advisors, and campus resources which served as a successful intervention.

DISCUSSION AND RECOMMENDATION

American colleges and universities go to great lengths to ensure that students make a seamless transition into the academic and social college environment. Unfortunately, these efforts fail to significantly impact the retention of Millennial African American male students. The programs and initiatives are broad in nature and general in scope. More focused and strategic efforts must be taken to address the specific needs and challenges faced by this population of students, instead of a one-size-fits-all approach. Colleges and universities must start using empirical data and research findings to guide these efforts instead of anecdotal information (Jafee, 2007). The findings from this study provided key factors that impact the first-year college experience of Millennial Black males. Because African American males come from a history of marginalization, discrimination, and a constant threat of negative stereotypes, considerable thought must be paid by educational leaders when constructing first-year programs for this student subgroup. These are a few recommendations developed based on this study and a review of the literature:

Conduct a men-only freshman workshop or orientation session. A gender-specific session would allow upperclassmen and administrators the opportunity to provide new freshman male students with support and could provide a forum for these stakeholders to make recommendations for institutional resources and programs geared toward their specific needs.

Provide an engaging social experience. Generate progressive and innovative social activities that not only foster a collaborative and interactive relationship with students, but also promote involvement in co-curricular activities and events. There should be a continuous emphasis on campus social activities and campus involvement (Shinde, 2010).

Establish a campus male student resource center. Consider allocating institutional resources to the development of a male student resource center that provides activities, tutors, workshops, and discussions that assist male students in unpacking issues surrounding the male college experience. The center can also include health services and aid in connecting students with male mentors.

Promote instructor-student relationships. Develop and promote interactive and collaborative instructor-student relationship. Formal and informal interaction can occur in and out of the classroom and can also incorporate hands-on experiential learning. Instructors can identify the best practices that engage male students such as varying instructional strategizes, learning students' names, taking field trips, encouraging co-curricular activities, and creating a firm but fair structured learning environment.

Higher education institutions can benefit greatly from constructing thoughtful and strategic approaches to engage and support African American male students during their first year. The retention and academic persistence of Black males are influenced by the techniques and strategies used to integrate them into the academic and social college environment. Encourage Black male students to participate in campus activities and events; construct learning experiences that provide opportunities for male bonding; facilitate male discussion groups; and solicit feedback from instructors, administrators, and students regarding the issues they face. Now that more Black males are enrolling in colleges and universities, the issue is not only about getting them in, but retaining them through to graduation. The landscape of the American educational system is fundamentally different than it was in the past, requiring that the recruitment and retention of Black males employ the efforts of the entire campus community.

REFERENCES

Burshong, S. (2009). Freshman retention drops, except at 2-year colleges. *Chronicle of Higher Education, 55*(21), A17.

Bush, E. C., & Bush, V. L. (2010, Feb/Mar). Calling out the elephant: An examination of African American male achievement in community college. *Journal of African American Males in Education, 1*(1), 40–62.

Dancy, T. E. (2011, July). Colleges in the making of manhood and masculinity: Gendered perspectives on African American males. *Gender and Education, 23*(4), 477–495.

Davis, J. E. (1995, November). *Campus climate, gender, and achievement of African-American college males.* Paper presented at the Annual Meeting of the Association for the Study of Higher Education, Orlando, FL.

Festinger, L. (1957). *A theory of cognitive dissonance.* Evanston, IL: Row, Peterson and Company.

Frierson, H., Pearson, W., & Wyche, J. H. (2009). *Black American males in higher education: Diminishing proportions.* Bingley, UK: Emerald Group.

Hilton, A. A., Wood, J. L., & Lewis, C. W. (2012). *Black males in postsecondary education: Examining their experiences in diverse institutional contexts.* Charlotte, NC: Information Age Pub.

Jafee, D. (2007). Peer cohorts and the unintended consequences of freshman learning communities. *College Teaching, 55*(2), 65–71.

Lowery, J. W. (2004). Student affairs for a new generation. *New Direction for Student Services, 106,* 87–98.

Mangan, K. (2014, March). Minority men struggle to achieve at community college. *Chronicle of Higher Education, 60*(25), A8.

Mangan, K. (2013, October). Stereotypes add to burden for male minority students, researcher says. *Chronicle of Higher Education, 60*(8), A1–A67.

Monaco, M., & Martin, M. (2007). The Millennial student: A new generation of learners. *Athletic Training Education Journal, 2,* 42–46.

Palmer, R. T., & Young, E. M. (2009, January). Determined to succeed: Salient factors that foster academic success for academically unprepared Black males at a Black college. *Journal of College Student Retention, 10*(4), 465–482.

Polite, V. C., & Davis, J. E. (1999). *African American males in school and society: Practices and policies for effective education.* New York, NY: Teachers College Press.

Rickes, P. C. (2009). Make way for Millennials! How today's students are shaping higher education space. *Planning for Higher Education, 37*(2), 7–17.

Roberts, J., & Styron, R. (2009). Student satisfaction and persistence: Factors vital to students. *Research in Higher Education Journal, 6,* 1–18.

Ross, T., Kena, G., Rathbun, A., Kewal Ramani, A., Zhang, J., Kristapovich, P., and Manning, E. (2012). *Higher education: Gaps in access and persistence study* (NCES 2012-046). U.S. Department of Education, National Center for Education Statistics. Washington, DC: Government Printing Office.

Schmidt, P. (2008). Colleges seek key to success of Black men in the classroom. *The Chronicle of Higher Education, 54*(A1), A23-25.

Scott, D., Havice, P., Livingston, W., & Cawthon, T. (2012). Men's identity development: Issues and implications for residence life. *Journal of College & University Student Housing, 38/39*(2/1), 200–213.

Seidman, A. (2012). *College student retention: Formula for student success* (2nd ed.). Lanham, MD: Rowman & Littlefield.

Shinde, G.S. (2010). The relationship between student's responses on the National Survey of Student Engagement and Retention. *Review of Higher Education and Self-Learning, 3*(7), 54–67.

Sieyes, P. (2008). Qualitative and quantitative research methods: Old wine in new bottles? *Paedagogica Historica, 44,* 691–705.

Signithia, F., & Ogbu, J. U. (1986). Black students' school success: Coping with the "burden of 'acting white.'" *The Urban Review, 18*(3), 176–206.

Simmons, L. D. (2013). Factors of persistence for African American men. *Journal of Negro Education, 82*(1), 62–74.

Strauss, W., & Howe, N. (2003). *Millennials go to college.* New York, NY: Quill.

Terrion, J. L., & Daoust, J. (2011). Assessing the impact of supplemental instruction on the retention of undergraduate students after controlling for motivation. *Journal of College Retention, Research, Theory and Practice, 13,* 311–327.

Tinto, V. (2006). Research and practice of student retention: What next? *Journal of College Retention, Research, Theory and Practice, 8,* 1–9.

Torisk, E. (2011, May). Generation Y heavily dependent on technology, promotes laziness. *The Jambar.* Retrieved from http://www.thejambar.com/generation-y-heavily-dependent-on-technology-promotes-laziness

Tucker, P. (2006). Teaching the Millennial generation. *The Futurist, 40*(3), 7.

Yin, R. K. (2009). *Case study research: Design and methods* (4th ed.). Thousand Oaks, CA: Sage.

CHAPTER TWO

Am I Not a Man and a Brother? I Am a Man

LaGARRETT KING

"Am I not a man and a brother?" and "I am a man" are slogans from different time periods in U.S. history that serve as examples of the contested terrain and questioning of Black manhood and masculinity. The first, "Am I not a man and a brother?" was the official seal of the British Society for the Abolition of Slavery in the late 1700s. This seal portrayed an enslaved African male in chains. He was kneeling in a submissive position, and it looked as if he were pleading to someone concerning his freedom.

"Am I Not a Man and a Brother?" Courtesy of the Library of Congress.

"I am a man"[1] was used during the Memphis sanitation workers strike of 1968 in protest of poor working conditions and low wages; over 200 workers marched through the city wearing signs reading "I am a man" over their chests.

Although they were used almost 200 years apart, these strikingly similar slogans both represented similar movements for Black male freedom and social equality. The first was created and employed by White abolitionists, and although their aim was to eradicate involuntary servitude, the image of the enslaved African indicated the paternal attitudes of White males to Black males. Estes (2005) noted that the seal revealed what "many white Americans, even abolitionists, expected African Americans to adopt; a submissive posture of supplication seeking emancipation" (p. 2). By framing the quest for manhood as a question, both the image and slogan elicited a type of deference to, or acknowledgment of, the White establishment.

On the other hand, "I am a man" employed a more forceful tone that rejected submissiveness and obsequiousness. Instead, in the spirit of the 1960s Civil

Rights Movement, Black men, tired of racial oppression, demanded that U.S. egalitarian values be extended to them. As one protester put it, the phrase "I am a man" simply meant "we ain't gonna take that shit no more" (Honey, 2008, p. 213). This slogan typifies the transition of Black men from waiting for the answer to "Am I not a man and a brother?" to declaring their own answer, "I am a man" (Estes, 2005, p. 2).

Throughout U.S. history, the contested depiction of Black masculinity has been defined, influenced, and juxtaposed against European standards of manhood and masculinity. Black men, however, have often exhibited agency and resisted superimposed notions of White masculinity by defining a diverse, complex, and multifaceted display of Black masculine identities (hooks, 2003; Hunter & Davis, 1994). Although these notions of "resistant masculinity" (Hine & Jenkins, 1999, p. 1) have arisen from the discourse on depictions of the Black man, this can be problematic, creating simplistic and normalized constructs of Black masculinity (Brown, 2011). Through written and visual media, the Black male body is read and portrayed in ways that allow society to misinterpret Black manhood and masculinity.

The purpose of this chapter is to interrogate various representations of Black male imagery. Using Anthony Brown's (2011) notion of Black male discourse and Richard Merelman's (1995) concept of Black cultural projections as guides, this chapter explores how a high school Black history textbook uses pictures to define Black manhood and masculinity. The textbook in question is Hine, Hine, and Harrold's (2011) *African-American History,* second edition, (Prentice Hall). Throughout the U.S., many school districts and states have special provisions to teach Black history as either part of their core curriculum or as an elective within social studies. As one of two Black history textbooks published by major textbook publishing companies (*African American History* by Lisbeth Gant-Britton (Holt, Rinehart and Winston is the second), it is difficult to determine how widespread its use and popularity have been. What makes *African-American History* interesting, however, is that the textbook has been adopted by the School District of Philadelphia, which is currently the only school district in the U.S. that mandates a yearlong course in Black history as a core graduation requirement (Janofsky, 2005). I conducted a content analysis of the textbook's pictures of Black males and used the following research question to guide my analysis: To what extent and in what ways do the images in Prentice Hall's *African-American History* demonstrate or challenge notions of Black manhood and masculinity?

This chapter has five sections. First, I explore the relevant literature on Black history, textbooks, and the way these texts portray Black manhood. Then I detail the frameworks that guide this study of imagery in *African-American History.* Next, I discuss the method and methodology that were used to examine Black male images. After the methods and methodology section, I note how Black male discourse and cultural projections are illustrated through the textbook. I conclude with thoughts regarding Black manhood and masculinity in school-based curriculum.

BLACK HISTORY, BLACK MEN, AND REVISIONIST ONTOLOGIES

Traditional approaches to Black history, or the lack thereof, in K-12 schools have had a long, contentious legacy. History education helps students begin to extrapolate their identity through narrative. They come to understand themselves, their community, their country, and other cultures by examining the past and relating this knowledge to the present. At all levels of the K-12 curriculum, the official narrative of America history favors Whiteness as a quintessential component of citizenship. The cultural groups and subgroups that threaten or do not measure up to these standards have been ignored or marginalized within the official curriculum. Black males often fall into this category.

Throughout the history of American curriculum and instruction, narratives have often been used to justify racial hierarchies and have constructed Black men as second-class citizens—naturally inferior to White men (Elson, 1964; Foster, 1999; King, Davis, & Brown, 2012; Reddick, 1934). More specifically, Black males have had a dual identity within this American historical narrative. Black males have been portrayed as docile, submissive, and childlike, while simultaneously represented as inherently violent, criminally inclined, and dangerous (Brown, 2010; Elson, 1964). These stereotyped images (Wynter, 1995) were used to justify surveillance and to control perceived threats of Black manhood and masculinity. Early textbooks depicted Black-skinned people as barbarians, destitute of intelligence, and having only a weak, suppressed sense of humanity (Brown, 2010; Elson, 1964; Foster, 1999). Traditional approaches to history taught that Black skin was cursed and its imagery promoted cultural, intellectual, and physical violence against Black males (Woodson, 2000). Woodson noted that the eradication of the history curriculum that taught Black inferiority was of great importance because "there would be no lynching if it did not start in the schoolroom" (p. 3).

Currently, the explicit and egregious language which demeaned Black people in historical textbooks is gone and Black history is more prevalent within history standards. There still persist, however, some problematic constructions of Black personhood in the official history curriculum. State and national standards continue to decontextualize, whitewash, and compress Black history into three historical eras: slavery, Reconstruction, and the Civil Rights Movement (Anderson & Metzger, 2011; Journell, 2008). In addition, only a few exceptional Black historical figures are included in the curriculum and are often only superficially addressed. The issues of institutionalized racism and oppression, and how they influenced the lived realities of Black people in the past and present, are superficially covered, if covered at all (Alridge, 2006; Brown & Brown, 2010; Carlson, 2003; Vasquez-Heilig, Brown, & Brown, 2012; Sleeter, 2002). Ladson-Billings (2003) posits that the history curriculum "present[s] an incoherent, disjointed picture of those who are not White" (p. 4). In other words, because of traditional history education, American society has limited knowledge of the collective experiences of Black males, who they are, their successes and failures, and how they perceive their manhood and masculinity.

Because of the general disjointed perception of Black history and identity, teaching Black history, for many people, has no academic, cultural, or theoretical value and is sometimes perceived as arbitrary, ceremonial, and ethnic cheerleading (Franklin et al., 1998; King, 1992; Nieto, 2005; King & Brown, 2012; Patterson, 1971). I contend that the typical Black history constructs ignore the essence of Black history. Since the creators of the past and present official history curriculum have had an incomplete understanding of the history and experience of Black people, Black history has come to serve as a counter-narrative to mainstream historical perspectives that have ignored or egregiously misrepresented the experiences of Black people generally. The chronicling of Black history was and continues to be a process whereby the limited and limiting constructs in typical history are problematized through a scientific process that revises, repudiates, and reimages the racial imagery of Black people—a process Mills (1998) called revisionist ontology.

Projects asserting Black history as revisionist ontology are designed to refute White-majority-imposed definitions of racial inferiority that are used to justify the second-class status of Blacks and sometimes the violent actions of Whites. School textbooks serve as one platform for redefinition. The emergence of Black history textbooks dates back to the mid-nineteenth century and includes textbooks written by influential educators and luminaries such as Edward A. Augusta, Lelia Amos Pendleton, Booker T. Washington, and Carter G. Woodson. Black historians, educators, and concerned citizens have written textbooks that present— through both textual and visual representations—Blackness, Black manhood, and Black masculinity in ways starkly different from traditional history textbooks. In this way, Black history textbooks became an important battleground for revisionist ontological work for Black men.

It is unclear if contemporary Black history textbooks, however, reflect the revisionist ontological approach of their predecessors. Few studies have explored the content of current Black history textbooks; this chapter fills this gap. Using the conceptual frameworks of Black male discourse and Black cultural projection, I investigate how a contemporary Black history textbook constructs Black manhood and masculinity through the use of pictures.

CONCEPTUAL AND THEORETICAL FRAMEWORKS

This chapter draws from the conceptual framework of Brown's (2011) Black male discourse and the theoretical framework of Merelman's (1995) Black cultural projection. Black male discourse is composed of the common and recycled stories that try to make sense of and explain the social and educational conditions of Black males (Brown, 2011). Brown noted that three types of narratives about Black males have been engrained in the social imagination and have served as a way to normalize Black male behavior. These discourses include Black males as absent and irresponsible fathers, people who are powerless to institutional structures of poverty and racism, and an endangered species in crisis.

The "absent and irresponsible" discourse developed as an attempt to explain Black males' new social and cultural behaviors in urban centers and Black family life in the early 1930s. Black males, as they transitioned from rural towns to urban cities, began to display behaviors that included "seamlessly wandering from place to place, seeking food, work, and shelter, but also engaging in loose sexual relations and carrying an eroded sense of family responsibility" (Brown, 2011, p. 2053). Black families suffered because fathers were absent and elusive, creating instability at home. Black families increasingly were headed by matriarchs, which signaled an abnormal and broken family structure. This instability negatively affected the Black family, especially the "social, emotional, and educational development of the Black male child" (Brown, 2011, p. 2054). Social scientists began to connect numerous problems within the Black community to this pervasive idea of the absent and irresponsible Black father.

The second narrative of Black male discourse is that they are powerless in the face of institutionalized structures of racism and poverty. This narrative connects the "vestiges of slavery and the macro-structural constraints of poverty, racial discrimination, and chronic joblessness" (Brown, 2011, p. 2056). These institutional and structural barriers in turn prevent Black men from being viewed as having attained manhood. Estes (2005) notes:

> Manhood entailed an economic, social, and political status ideally achievable by all men. A man was the head of his household: he made enough money to support his family as the primary if not the only breadwinner. He also had a political voice in deciding how his community, his state, and his country were run. (p. 7)

When Black men are unable to achieve these standards of manhood, emasculation ensues. Due to racist employment practices and union policies during the early to middle years of the 20th century, Black men struggled to attain high-paying jobs. Black men, in turn, often felt their economic situation was hopeless. Black women continued to be the heads of household, but this narrative makes them complicit in the emasculation of Black men as well as the boys they raise. Since Black women are the only or dominant parental figures in the majority of Black households, Black boys have limited male role models to teach them how to be a man. Black boys in turn reject "appropriate" conceptions of manhood. This discourse stresses that Black males feel powerless because they are incapable of being fathers, husbands, and providers, and their power resides in seeking alternative affirmations of Black manhood.

The third narrative maintains that Black men are an endangered species and in crisis, a belief which developed throughout the 1980s to explain the social and educational conditions of Black males. The focus here was not on institutional conditions of racism, but on the psychological effects of racism on Black male behavior. This narrative maintains that the Black male has a dysfunctional image of himself, which has led to a damaged psyche. Once again, Black masculinity is reframed apart from traditional, mainstream hegemonic masculinity, being classified as "self-destructive," "life threatening," "psychologically brutalizing," and as a "critical psychological [defense] to ward off racial oppression and social inequality" (Brown, 2011, p. 2065). Black males are seen as overcompensating through toughness, sexual promiscuity, and overt violence to resolve interpersonal conflict (Brown, 2011). These masculine behaviors are seen as a mechanism to cope with the natural alienation caused by racism.

These narratives attempt to inform scholars, educators, and policy makers about the socio-psychological and the material conditions of Black males in the United States. These axioms became part of a long and recursive discourse that has normalized or provided what Brown (2011) called "common sense narratives" or "universal stories" (p. 2049) to explain why Black males exhibit certain behaviors and have problems integrating in society. These narratives are systemically held together through a social apparatus that includes the media, popular cultural, and education.

This nexus of racism creates an image of Black men that disassociates them from notions of manhood defined by White, middle-class, American norms. Although these narratives are persistent in how American society imagines Black males, there have been efforts to promote an alternative vision of Black masculinity. One such effort is exhibited through Merelman's (1995) framework, Black cultural projection. Black cultural projection is the conscious or unconscious effort of Black people and their allies to place new, more positive images of themselves before dominant groups, for the purpose of increasing their own cultural capital (p. 3). Black cultural projections are born out of the understanding that dominant groups strategically make use of discriminatory or stereotyped images in order to maintain racial hierarchy. Black cultural projections empower subordinate groups with the agency to create new and alternative discourses that challenge negative constructions.

Merelman's (1995) four concepts regarding Black cultural projections are: syncretism, hegemony, polarization, and counter-hegemony. Syncretism is classified as the "union of different and opposing principles" (p. 5) and is applied when both dominant and subordinate groups come to a consensus on a certain projection, which Merelman describes as mutual cultural projection. The second cultural projection is hegemony, which occurs when dominant groups control the cultural projection. The subordinate viewpoint is silenced while the dominant viewpoint is the only projection deemed salient, typically being deemed intrinsically true or "common sense." The third cultural projection is polarization, which is when the dominant group projection and Black cultural projection are equal in prominence, though diametrically opposed. The fourth cultural projection is counter-hegemony, which is the mode when the dominant group becomes more accepting of the subordinate group's cultural projection and begins to accept and question power structures, including their privilege.

In my examination of *African-American History*, I juxtapose these two frameworks. I began by cataloging each picture in the text and coding for whether it represented Black manhood in terms of absenteeism, powerlessness, or endangerment. Through my analysis, I was able to understand *African-American History*'s positioning of Black manhood and masculinity. In this context, the three narratives of Black male discourse are problematic in terms of constructing Black manhood. Representations of Black masculinity aligned to these narratives produced a cultural projection that was hegemonic and polarizing to Black male identity. If *African-American History* continues the revisionist ontological tradition of Black history, their narratives and images should uphold counter-hegemonic viewpoints regarding Black males.

METHODOLOGY

For this study, I employed a critical visual methodology with a special emphasis on content analysis (Rose, 2011). Rose (2011) notes that critical visual methodology:

> [thinks] about the visual in terms of [its] cultural significance, social practices and power relations in which it is embedded; and that means thinking about the power relations that produce, are articulated through and can be challenged by, ways of seeing and imaging. (p. xv)

Instead of passively looking at pictures without context, it is important to critically understand the visual through what Rose termed social modality. Social modality "refers to the range of economic, social, and political relations, institutions and practices that surround an image and through which it is seen and used" (p. 13). Visuals—in this case, textbook pictures—are not neutral, fixed, or stable documents that transmit limited meaning; instead, pictures are situated within a "network of interactions" (Prior, 2003) that are interpreted based on their own visual effects, social context, and the audience's positionality. Interpretation, therefore, occurs at three different points: where the image was produced, where the image is situated, and the primary site where audiences make meaning (Rose, 2011). The last is of great importance to this study and has major influence over how textbook visuals are understood.

Understanding how the audience makes meaning from textbooks is important because of the mechanism's unique position as the authority of official knowledge. Scholars (Anyon, 1979; Apple, 2000) have long purported that school textbooks are political apparatuses that instill ideological conditioning about certain beliefs and practices and exclude historically marginalized communities. Apple (2000) notes that textbooks "signify through their content and form, particular ways of selecting and organizing" (p. 46). This is exhibited through the prominence of the dominant culture's viewpoints throughout the text, which provides more cultural capital to the dominant culture and continuing the subjugation of historically marginalized groups. Because this analysis focuses on a Black history textbook, it provides a unique examination due to the expected differences in historical approach and legitimacy of its portrayal of Black narratives as opposed to traditional history textbooks. In other words, Black history textbooks should provide a more diverse, inclusive, and critical narrative regarding Black historical figures and events than traditional textbooks.

The content analysis of the visual representation of Black manhood and masculinity required four steps. The first step involved locating specific pictures to analyze. Using stratified sampling (Rose, 2011), I conducted a page-by-page assessment of the textbook to identify pictures that featured Black males. I located 210 pictures that include Black males. The second step was creating a coding scheme matrix based on the Black male discourse conceptual framework. I used the codes *AI* for absent and irresponsible, *PL* for powerless, and *EC* for endangered and in crisis. The third step involved using the coding scheme to evaluate the pictures selected. I looked for certain aspects of the picture to match them with the code.

For example, for *AI*, I looked for pictures that illustrate Black males in family roles, as fathers, husbands, or as role models. I also considered pictures that feature Black males as community leaders or serving the public through government service. Pictures that represent Black women as heads of family were also coded as *AI* because of the theme's focus on absentee males in homes. Pictures coded *PL* depicted Black men exhibiting agency through serving in positions of power in the community, general society, government, and the military. Any pictures that illustrated Black males in despair were also coded *PL*. For the last code, *ES*, I looked for pictures that illuminate Black male suffering or attempting to rectify wrongs caused by institutionalized barriers throughout society. The dichotomy between the two depictions illustrates that although Black males were engulfed in a discourse of dysfunction, a counter-narrative to the endangered discourse is Black male agency that attempts to rectify society's wrongdoings.

I coded each picture based on how these images re-inscribed or responded to Brown's narratives of Black male discourse. Through this process, I selected the coded pictures and grouped them together, noting the textual explanation in the book chapter or the caption under the picture itself. Sixteen pictures were coded as *AI*, 75 were coded *PL*, and 12 coded as *ES*. The sections that follow explore how the pictures in *African-American History* respond to the narratives of Brown's Black male discourse.

The last step of analysis was comparing the common themes of the conceptual framework in relation to the discourse of Black manhood. This is important because it allows the researcher to "understand the document in relation to their milieu or social context" (McCulloch, 2004, p. 6). This process allowed me to go beyond simply focusing on the visual representation of Black males in this Black history textbook. The theoretical framework allowed me to analyze the visuals within their social modality and explicitly note how they responded to Black male discourse.

BLACK CULTURAL PROJECTIONS: ABSENT AND IRRESPONSIBLE

Consistent throughout *African-American History* is a focus on Black family life. The book indicates that Black families, including the father, value marriage and family life. In the chapter section "Slave Life," under "Marriage," the book notes that Black slave households did not align with "Southern White concepts of patriarchy," which required male dominance (Hine et al., 2011, p. 160). Instead, Black families during this time were partnerships, with both spouses as equals. The textbook also emphasizes that slavery did not stop Black men from being salient parts of their family's life. During enslavement, Black fathers lived in one-room dwellings with their families, and men who lived outside of their wives' plantation visited the family in the evening after the workday.

In the section entitled "The Great Migration," under "Families," Black men are portrayed as responsible family men. The book notes that "most northern Black families, although hardly well to do, were two-parent households. Women headed comparatively few families. Fathers were present in seven of ten black families in New York City in 1925" (p. 467). Although there is no accompanying illustration, the text establishes that, in opposition to the dominant absent-and-irresponsible narrative, Black men were in actuality not absent from the household and or neglecting their familial responsibilities. Despite the circumstances, many attempted to be good fathers, providers, and husbands. This theme is demonstrated in several pictures throughout the book. For example, "A Pastoral Visit" (p. 168 in *African-American History*) portrays a poor Black family with a Black father. "A Pastoral Visit" is a painting featuring the father, mother, and their three children sitting around the dinner table with a guest, a pastor from the community. In the picture, the wife is serving food to the guest, while the pastor (sitting at the head of the table), and the father (to the right) are having a conversation. Two children are listening to the conversation either waiting for food to be served or to be dismissed from the table. The illustration seems to depict the father as a hardworking man (tattered clothes and work boots) with a close relationship with the children. For example, one of his children is bending down on his knee, looking as though she (indicted by the dress) is sleeping, crying, or waiting to be held, showing the intimacy between father and child. Another indicator of a close family bond and the father's status in the family is the guitar near the front of the dinner table next to the father. By placing the guitar close to the father and during family dinner may indicate a favorite family event or tradition, led by the father. The conversation with a local pastor at dinner, the intimate action of the youngest child waiting patiently for her father's affection, and the family guitar are indicators of a specific rendering of Black fatherhood that runs counter to the discourse of the absentee father.

Another example of Black family life in *African-American History* is the photograph, "Three Generations of an African American Family," which was originally featured in the 1900 Paris World's Fair in W. E. B. Du Bois's exhibit, "The American Negro."

Negro Life in Georgia. Photo Album, vol. 4, ca. 1900. Print and Photographs Division. Library of Congress. Bequest of Daniel A. P. Murray, ca. 1926 (42.7) Digital ID# ppmsca-08762.

Juxtaposed with "A Pastoral Visit," this picture features what looks to be a middle-class (as evidenced by their attire and posture) Black family. Sitting on a lawn, the family consists of a grandmother, the mother, two children (a boy and a girl), and the father, who is positioned in the middle. Each person is dressed in formal attire; the father and son are in suits with bowties and the ladies wear long skirts and blouses. The picture represents a type of Black fatherhood that shows the family's deference to the father. The father is a powerful figure. This is represented through his position as the centerpiece of the picture and through his bearing, his upright, stoic posture which indicates confidence. In addition, his daughter's action of draping her hands over his shoulders illustrates respect, kinship, and high regard for him as a father.

African-American History displays Black fatherhood in several ways. These illustrations of family intimacy posit a discourse that Black fathers were active participants in their children's lives and were not irresponsible people who carried "an eroded sense of family responsibility" (Brown, 2011, p. 2053). The pictures imply that Black males of this period were indeed accountable for their family's lives; this is illustrated through the amount of deference and intimacy the children show to their fathers. Obvious affection and tenderness do not signal an absentee father but rather acknowledge the sacrifice and dedication the father exerts towards one's family. Other pictures display Black males as loving husbands, brothers, protectors and providers, as well as community leaders and activists (see pages 166, 223, 242, 318, 389, 466 in *African-American History*). Indeed, the pictures in this text counter the Black male absentee narrative and provide a cultural projection that Black males were present and respected figures in their households and communities.

BLACK CULTURAL PROJECTIONS: POWERLESS

African-American History responds to the powerless Black male discourse in several ways. The most common way is through biographical accounts of esteemed Black male figures throughout the book. While some may argue that Black male text features are part of marginalizing knowledge (King, 2004), or are contributionist narratives (Banks, 2004; Patterson, 1971), the biographic sections highlight Black males who had to cope with racism and poverty rather than only the handful of exceptional Black historical figures who commonly appear in history books. These illustrations indicate that Black males did not accept their imposed subordinate positions and refute the notion that they were somehow psychologically damaged and powerless. Instead, they used their struggle as a mechanism to realize their inherent power.

Paul Robeson as Othello.

For instance, the picture of Paul Robeson as Othello is accompanied by text that explains that his father was a slave, but he was able to go to college, obtain success thereafter, and become one of the foremost voices of the Civil Rights Movement. He eventually was blacklisted for his activism during the age of McCarthyism, but remained a staunch supporter of Black equality and equity and continued to fight for what was right. Another picture, Randall Robinson (p. 681), is accompanied by a narrative that explains briefly how he overcame segregated public school experiences and became a top Boston attorney and founding executive director of TransAfrica in 1977. His involvement with TransAfrica helped him fight against South Africa's apartheid system. He was also the author of *The Debt: What America Owes to Blacks* (2000).

Another example of how the powerless discourse is rejected in *African-American History* is its portrayal of the position of Black soldiers. Pictures illustrating Black males in the military included "African-American Soldiers" (p. 416), "Lieutenant Colonel Charles D. Young" below, "The World War II Department Recruitment Poster" (p. 573), and "Two American Orderlies" (p. 574). Although the text notes that most "Black units served in auxiliary roles" (p. 416) because of racial discrimination and other structural policies in the armed services, these pictures feature Black males as instrumental in the struggle for U.S. democracy.

Major Charles Young with officers in Mexico. Source: US Cavalry, NPS; public doman.

The powerless discourse is challenged by two facts. First, by joining the U.S. armed forces, Black males were exerting their power and responding to problematic discourses which asserted that they were mentally or physically inferior and unfit for duty. Second, deciding to join was not about blind patriotism or favoring U.S. interests: there persisted a larger purpose for Black male military service in the form of full citizenship rights (Brown, Crowley, & King, 2011; Nash, 2013). Whether joining the army during the American Revolution or during World War II, Black males were fighting for full equality for the race.

What these pictures and the accompanying text represent with regard to the powerlessness discourse is that not all Black males identified with that stereotype. These biographical accounts counter the discourse concerning Black males' psychological condition in the face of racism and poverty as hopeless. *African-American History* elicits a cultural projection that all Black males did not resort to deviant behaviors because the system was against them. Instead, Black males, in many cases, used the system for their benefit. Pictures featuring Black male achievement and Black military men are mainly about agency in displaying their power and not idly sitting by and accepting the institutional constraints of racism or poverty. In other words, the cultural projection of Black males in the text is one of power as opposed to powerlessness and establishes Black male agency as an essential aspect of Black male identity.

BLACK CULTURAL PROJECTIONS: ENDANGERED AND IN CRISIS

African-American History responds to the endangered and in crisis discourse in two ways. The first is to explicitly present the atrocities against Black males in society throughout U.S. history. The second is to show Black male agency to improve conditions of the race. Instead of the focus being on the destructive behavior of Black males, the textbook pictures represent the actions to curtail or rectify some of the institutional racism and oppression endured by Black males in U.S. society.

First, several events are highlighted to represent Black males as endangered or in crisis. These include pictures of the Scottsboro Boys , Emmett Till , and the Rodney King incident . What these pictures represent are several discourses that illustrate the dangers to Black masculinity in U.S. society. Beginning with the Scottsboro boys and Emmett Till's representation, we see a dichotomous view of Black childhood. We see the youthful innocence and jubilance of Emmett Till with his mother, but despite the fact the prisoners are well-groomed and nicely clothed, we notice the hard and joyless exterior of the Scottsboro Boys. While these pictures may elicit different reactions, the Scottsboro Boys and Emmett Till pictures and their stories represent similar aspects of the threat to Black masculinity and sexuality.

Ms. Juanita E. Jackson visiting the Scottsboro Boys, January 1937. Library of Congress Prints and Photographs Division. Visual Materials from the NAACP records (reproduction number LC-USZ62-123456).

Emmett Till and his mother, Mamie Bradley, ca. 1955. Gelatin Silver Print. Visual Materials from the NAACP Records, Prints and Photographs Division, Library of Congress (7). Courtesy of the NAACP. Digital ID: cph 3f06304.

Fear of the Black male threat manifested in the accusation of rape and the accusation of perceived and forbidden admiration of a White woman (Sommerville, 1995; Duru, 2004). The innocence and purity of the White woman and White men's responsibility to protect her virtue from the stereotypical danger of Black male sexuality have been used for justification for violence against Black men. Lynching and castrating were used to control the perceived sexual transgressions inherent to the Black male. The Scottsboro Boys, who were accused of rape, and Emmett Till, who said "Bye, baby" to a shop owner's wife, appear in the textbook as examples of this harmful discourse. All but one Scottsboro Boy was initially sentenced to death, and Emmett Till was kidnapped, tortured, mangled, shot, and drowned.

Rodney King represents another angle of the discourse of the Black male menace. The discourse of Black men as violent and criminally inclined has been used as an explanation for their overrepresentation in prisons and police brutality. In the photo below, King can be seen on the ground while one police officer swings his club with his fellow officers watching. The video from which this picture was taken would reveal that several of the officers took turns hitting King until he was unconscious.

Rodney King and L.A. police. CNN via Getty Images.

The officers were not convicted in the criminal case, as the story surrounding King portrayed him as a violent and dangerous aggressor whom the police had the right to subdue, control, and correct. Thus, the text addresses head-on the violent injustices suffered by Black men throughout U.S. history as a result of the pervasive but inaccurate stereotype that they are all innately violent, overly sexual, and menacing. The text engages with the discourse that Black men are in crisis by highlighting that the crisis is a not result of fatal flaws intrinsic to Black males, but was created by a normalized racism which demonizes Black men and masculinity.

Another way *African-American History* responds to the endangered narrative is by presenting pictures that extoll the agency of Black males attempting to change the current status of the race. Pictures such as "Roosevelt's Black Cabinet" (p. 520) and The Founders of the Niagara Movement (p. 439) represent Black male agency to create a better life for Black citizens. The Black Cabinet—an unofficial name—

was a group of 27 Black men and women who were considered "race specialists" and "pressured the president [F. D. Roosevelt] and the heads of federal agencies to adopt and support colorblind policies and lobbied to advance the status of Black Americans" (Hine et al., 2011, p. 520). Headed by W. E. B. Du Bois, the Niagara Movement was a gathering of Black and White activists who wanted to end discrimination against Black people. That movement served as a precursor of the NAACP.

African-American History reinscribes Black males as endangered and in crisis, challenging the endangered discourse by implying that Black males are threatened by society, rather than endangered because of their own anti-social behavior. The endangered and in crisis narrative is embedded within the collective memory of society, perpetuated by hegemonic White fear. Various pictures throughout the text warn that for Black males, sometimes it does not matter if you were defending yourself, in need of medical attention, exhibiting childish behavior, or being stopped for a traffic violation—your life as a Black man is endangered because you live in a society that has demonized you for your Blackness and your maleness, has already judged you a threat, and treats you accordingly. The narrative is challenged through pictures that show Black male agency. Pictures of the Black Cabinet and Niagara Movement portray Black men who attempted to change these prevailing negative images.

CONCLUSION

African-American History serves as a counter-hegemonic Black cultural projection for Black manhood and masculinity. Even narratives that reinscribed notions of the endangered narrative represent it more as a societal deficiency, recognizing historical oppression, and providing a caution to Black males about the narrow and egregious stereotypes that mar their conception of self and society's perception of them. The text represents an alternative discourse of Black manhood and masculinity. The focus, however, is not about how "positive" some of the projections are throughout the text. Instead, the textbook helps school children critically think about Black male identity, institutional racism, oppression, and ideology, and also how masculinity and manhood have been performed and controlled in varied spaces throughout history.

Examining the cultural projection of Black males in *African-American History* is important because it represents a counter-hegemonic rendering of Black manhood and masculinity that can be presented to school children. Throughout society, citizens are bombarded with recursive discourses and images that have constructed Black manhood and masculinity as something foreign, abnormal, or inherently deficient. Today we are continuously reminded about the problems with Black boys in the United States (Noguera, 2009). Discourses about the epidemic of fatherless Black families, more Black men in prison than in college, the failures of Black boys in schools, and successful Black people "acting White" have prevailed in our society for decades. We know that there are some serious issues concerning Black males and the community; but these discourses are incomplete and do not tell the entire story. Black manhood and some of the problems associated with Black men are sensationalized in society and constructed as the Black males' fault while larger contextual, sociological, and psychological factors are either ignored or marginalized.

Although traditional textbooks do not explicitly promote these negative discourses, the silence about Black history is complicit in the perpetuation of these negative perceptions of Black manhood or masculinity. *African-American History* presents a unique approach to history education and the construction of Black manhood and masculinity because of its polarizing and counter-hegemonic portrayals of Black males throughout history. What is of great importance is the ability of history to help people understand the contemporary world. *African-American History*'s greatest value is what Trouillot (1995) calls historical authenticity. *African-American History* is certainly concerned with what historical knowledge is taught throughout the course, but there is a larger purpose in how the textbook illustrates the ways that the "present re-presents the past" (Trouillot, 1995, p. 148). How do students, teachers, and educational stakeholders learn about current conceptions of Black masculinity and respond to the societal implications of these beliefs? Illustrations that picture Black males performing varied constructions of masculinity help Black males in particular to visualize not only who they are in terms of these textbook illustrations, but also who they could become (Wallace & Smith, 2012). This presents a more nuanced understanding of Black manhood and masculinity and problematizes limiting notions of Black manhood.

Returning back to the slogans with which I introduced the historical dimensions of Black manhood and masculinity, *African-American History* does not passively question "Am I not a man and a brother?"; instead, the textbook continues the tradition of demanding respect and acknowledgment of different conceptualizations of Black manhood and masculinity. The textbook's visuals and text state "I am a man" by presenting Black male diversity and experiences throughout U.S. history. With over 200 pictures of Black manhood throughout the book, a counter-hegemonic voice arises that rejects antiquated and racist definitions of Black manhood and masculinity and challenges us, Black males, to instead rely on ourselves to define, redefine, and reclaim our humanity.

NOTE

1. See the Ernest Withers Collection, http://www.thewitherscollection.com/civil.php

REFERENCES

Alridge, D. (2006). The limits of master narratives in history textbooks: An analysis of representations of Martin Luther King, Jr. *The Teachers College Record, 108*(4), 662–686.
Anderson, C. B., & Metzger, S. A. (2011). Slavery, the Civil War era, and African American representation in U.S. history: An analysis of four states' academic standards. *Theory & Research in Social Education, 39*(3), 393–415. doi: 10.1080/00933104.2011.10473460
Anyon, J. (1979). Ideology and United States history textbooks. *Harvard Educational Review, 49*(3), 361–386.
Apple, M. W. (2000). *Official knowledge: Democratic education in a conservative age* (2nd ed.). New York, NY: Routledge.
Banks, J. (2004). Multicultural education: Historical development, dimensions, and practice. In J. A. Banks & C. A. McGee (Eds.), *Handbook of research in multicultural education* (pp. 50–65). San Francisco, CA: Jossey-Bass.
Brown, A. L. (2010). Counter-memory and race: An examination of African American scholars' challenges to twentieth century K-12 historical discourse. *The Journal of Negro Education, 79*(1), 54–65.
Brown, A. L. (2011). Same old stories: The black male in social science and educational literature, 1930s to the present. *Teachers College Record, 113*(9), 2047–2079.
Brown, A. L., & Brown, K. D. (2010). Strange fruit indeed: Interrogating contemporary textbook representations of racial violence toward African Americans. *Teachers College Record, 112*(1), 31–67.
Brown, A. L., Crowley, R. M., & King, L. J. (2011). Black Civitas: An examination of Carter Woodson's contributions to teaching about race, citizenship, and the Black soldier. *Theory & Research in Social Education, 39*, 278–299. doi:10.1080/ 00933104.2011.10473455
Carlson, D. (2003). Troubling heroes: Of Rosa Parks, multicultural education, and critical pedagogy. *Cultural Studies <=> Critical Methodologies, 3*(1), 44–61. doi: 10.1177/1532708603239267
Duru, N. J. (2004). The Central Park Five, the Scottsboro Boys, and the myth of the bestial Black man. *Cardozo Law Review, 25*, 1315–1365.
Elson, R. (1964). *Guardians of tradition: American schoolbooks of the nineteenth century*. Lincoln, NE: University of Nebraska Press.
Estes, S. (2005). *I am a man!: Race, manhood, and the Civil Rights Movement*. Chapel Hill, NC: University of North Carolina Press.
Foster, S. J. (1999). The struggle for American identity: Treatment of ethnic groups in United States history textbooks. *History of Education, 28*(3), 251–227.
Franklin, J., Horne, G., Cruse, H., Ballard, A., & Reavis, L. (1998). Serious truth telling or a triumph in tokenism? *Journal of Black People in Higher Education, 18*, 87–92.
Hine, D. C., & Jenkins, E. (Eds.). (1999). *A question of manhood: A reader in U.S. Black men's history and masculinity* (Vol. 1). Bloomington, IN: Indiana University Press.
Hine, D. C., Hine, W. C., & Harrold, S. (2011). *African-American History* (2nd ed.). Boston, MA: Prentice Hall.
Honey, M. K. (2008). *Going down Jericho Road: The Memphis Strike, Martin Luther King's last campaign*. New York, NY: W. W. Norton & Company.
hooks, b. (2003). *We real cool: Black men and masculinity*. New York, NY: Routledge.
Hunter, A. G., & Davis, J. E. (1994). Hidden voices of Black men: The meaning, structure, and complexity of manhood. *Journal of Black Studies, 25*(1), 20–40.

Janofsky, M. A. (2005, July 25). Philadelphia mandates Black History for graduation. *The New York Times*. Retrieved from http://www.nytimes.com/

Journell, W. (2008). When oppression and liberation are the only choices: The representation of African-Americans within state social studies standards. *Journal of Social Studies Research, 32*(1), 40–50.

King, J. E. (1992). Diaspora literacy and consciousness in the struggle against miseducation in the Black community. *Journal of Negro Education, 61*(3), 317–340.

King, J. E. (2004). Culture-centered knowledge: Black studies, curriculum transformation, and social action. In J. Banks & C. Banks (Eds.), *Handbook of research on multicultural education* (2nd ed.), (pp. 349–378). San Francisco, CA: Jossey-Bass.

King, L. J., & Brown, A. L. (2012). Black History, Inc.! Investigating the production of Black History through Walmart's corporate website. *Multicultural Perspectives, 14*(1), 4–10. doi: 10.1080/15248372.2012.646633

King, L., Davis, C., & Brown, A. (2012). African American history, race and textbooks: An examination of the works of Harold O. Rugg and Carter G. Woodson. *Journal of Social Studies Research, 36*(4), 359–386.

Ladson-Billings, G. (2003). *Critical race theory perspectives on social studies: The profession, policies, and curriculum*. Greenwich, CT: Information Age.

McCulloch, G. (2004). *Documentary research: In education, history, and the social sciences*. New York, NY: Routledge.

Merelman, R. M. (1995). *Representing Black culture: Race and cultural politics in the United States*. New York, NY: Routledge.

Mills, C. (1998). Revisionist ontologies: Theorizing White supremacy. In C. Mills (Ed.), *Blackness visible: Essays on philosophy and race*. Ithaca, NY: Cornell University Press.

Nash, G. B. (2013). The African Americans' revolution. In E. G. Gray & J. Kamensky (Eds.), *The Oxford handbook of the American Revolution* (pp. 250–272). New York, NY: Oxford University Press.

Nieto, S. (2005). School reform and student learning: A multicultural perspectives. In J. A. Banks & C. A. Banks (Eds.), *Multicultural education: Issues and perspectives* (5th ed.), (pp. 401–420). Hoboken, NJ: John Wiley & Sons.

Noguera, P. A. (2009). *The trouble with Black boys: And other reflections on race, equity, and the future of public education*. San Francisco, CA: Jossey-Bass.

Patterson, O. (1971). Rethinking Black history. *Harvard Educational Review, 41*, 297–315

Prior, L. (2003). *Using documents in social research*. London, UK: Sage.

Reddick, L. (1934). Racial attitudes in American history textbooks of the south. *The Journal of Negro History, 19*, 225–265.

Robinson, R. (2000). *The debt: What America owes to Blacks*. New York, NY: Dutton Books.

Rose, G. (2011). *Visual methodologies: An introduction to researching with visual materials*. Thousand Oaks, CA: Sage.

Sleeter, C. E. (2002). State curriculum standards and student consciousness. *Social Justice, 29*(4): 8–25.

Sommerville, D. M. (1995). The rape myth in the old South reconsidered. *The Journal of Southern History, 61*(3), 481–518.

Trouillot, M. R. (1995). *Silencing the past: Power and the production of history*. Boston, MA: Beacon Press.

Vasquez-Heilig, J. V., Brown, K. D., & Brown, A. L. (2012). The illusion of inclusion: A critical race theory textual analysis of race and standards. *Harvard Educational Review, 82*(3), 403–424.

Wallace, M. O., & Smith, S. M. (2012). *Pictures and progress: Early photography and the making of African American identity*. Durham, NC: Duke University Press.

Woodson, C. G. (2000). *The miseducation of the Negro*. Trenton, NJ: Africa World Press. (Original work published 1933).

Wynter, S. (1995). 1492: A new world view. In V. Lawrence & R. Nettleford Winant (Eds.), *Race, discourse and the origin of the Americas: A new world view* (pp. 5–57). Washington, DC: Smithsonian Institution Press.

CHAPTER THREE

All Eyes on Me: High-Profile African American Male Student-Athletes' Social Transition Into Predominantly White Institutions of Higher Education

DARREN D. KELLY

African American male student-athletes are perhaps the most recognizable students at predominantly White NCAA Division I institutions. While their prominence is already high because they are one of the most visible historically underrepresented groups on campus, they are also frequently featured on television, radio, Internet, and other media outlets, making them stand out even more (Person, Benson-Quaziena, & Rogers, 2001). Despite accounting for only 9% of the total males enrolled in NCAA Division I colleges and universities, African American male student-athletes make up 30% of all the male student-athletes on athletic scholarship (NCAA, 2014a). Often, the most common image of the African American male student is the African American male student-athlete. Thus, due to their prominence in the media and campus culture, the choices they make and the things they do both on and off the field or court are highlighted and criticized openly and often.

Much of the prior literature on African American male student-athletes has suggested that these individuals have been exploited for their athletic ability and that their athletic participation often hinders their ability to reap many of the positive educational benefits of attending college (Edwards, 1984; Eitzen, 2009; Hawkins, 2001; Sailes, 1986). Scholars have used a number of theoretical frameworks to explain why academic outcomes are hindered. For example, a number of scholars have employed conflict theory to explain the reason for the academic issues of student-athletes in the major revenue-producing sports of football and basketball, where African American males are overrepresented (Eitzen, 2001; Patterson, 2000). Eitzen (2009) and Hawkins (2001) argue that the commercialization of and money invested in major college athletics has driven increased pressure on student-athletes to focus the bulk of their time, energy, and attention on athletics, while making academic responsibilities an afterthought. Another common framework utilized to explain the academic performance of student-athletes is a social psychological framework. This framework focuses on micro-level issues such as identity, role conflict, and stereotype threat, and how they affect the academic progress of African American male student-athletes (Benson, 2000; Harrison, Harrison, & Moore, 2002; Steele, 1997). More recently, scholars have used interest convergence and Critical Race Theory (CRT) to help explain why African American male student-athletes are encouraged to participate in revenue-generating sports for the purpose of creating wealth and bragging rights for predominantly White institutions, while not stressing academic pursuits and graduation that would benefit the athlete (Donnor, 2005; Hodge, Burden, Robinson, & Bennett III, 2008; Singer, 2005).

Hawkins (2001) utilized an internal colonization model to illustrate the academic and noncognitive struggles that African American student-athletes faced on predominantly White campuses. Using data from the American Institute for Research's (1989) *Report #3: The experiences of Black Intercollegiate Athletes at NCAA Division I Institutions*, Hawkins compared Black student-athletes to colonized individuals in order to illustrate the potential exploitation of this group as migrant labor. According to Hawkins, Black student-athletes experienced racial and social isolation, sensed that they were different from other students, felt a lack of control over their lives, and encountered racial discrimination. Essentially, these factors contributed to a lack of academic success amongst African American male student-athletes and were grounds for total reform of the intercollegiate athletic system.

In addition to the academic struggles of African American male student-athletes and African American football players in particular (due to their status as arguably the most visible student-athletes on large college campuses), there are numerous psychosocial and cultural issues these young men face in institutions of higher learning. Hyatt (2003) highlighted that commitment, discrimination, and isolation were some of the major barriers for African American male student-athletes as they pursued a quality overall college experience. First, African

American student-athletes' commitment to their sport is typically at odds with their commitment to their academics; additionally, these individuals have difficulty merging long-term career and life interests with short-term athletic career opportunities. Further, their extensive athletic commitments also lead to isolation, since African American male student-athletes are often less integrated into campus life and the academic setting. Last, African American student-athletes have expressed that they feel discriminated against by other faculty and students because of their race and the perceived privilege of their status as college athletes (especially in revenue-based sports).

LACK OF ACADEMIC PREPARATION AMONG AFRICAN AMERICAN MALE STUDENT-ATHLETES

While a number of frameworks have been utilized to investigate and explain the academic performance of African American male student-athletes, academic preparedness prior to enrollment in college remains a major issue for many of these individuals. Harry Edwards, in his (1984) article "The Black 'Dumb Jock': An American Sports Tragedy," argued that African American student-athletes were the least prepared for college compared to other student-athletes and students on campus. This was primarily because many of the recruited Black athletes came from economically disadvantaged communities with poor schools and little resources to fully prepare students for college. Other scholars have acknowledged that this trend has continued for decades into the 21st century (Benson, 2000; Eitzen & Purdy, 1986).

Due in part to the prevalent social and economic issues in the African American community, many African American children receive little academic preparation in their early years, leading to poor academic performance in primary and secondary schools. African American students rank at the bottom of many of the educational measures and indicators at various levels of primary and secondary education (Carter & Welner, 2013). In 2011, the average SAT scores of African American males were lower than average scores of all genders and ethnicities in reading and writing, while their math scores were lowest of all groups except African American females (College Board, 2011). African American males are lagging behind males and females of other races and ethnicities in their academic preparedness and college readiness. Thus, many African American males struggle with their transition into college after a deficient secondary education. Combined with other social factors, including participation in athletics, African American males are primed to struggle in their adjustment to the collegiate environment.

Frustration at home and in the classroom may be among the factors that lead African American boys to channel their energy into athletic pursuits. Since many Black young men see excellence in academics as acting White and not aligned with Black masculinity as portrayed in the media, they turn to athletics as their best path towards career success and financial gain. Additionally, many perceive other more lucrative and less competitive jobs and careers as unavailable to them and view athletics as an arena where they can win and achieve acclaim and praise.

THE NEED FOR INNOVATION IN ASSISTING AFRICAN AMERICAN MALE STUDENT-ATHLETES

Since NCAA Division I athletic departments do not seem to be making any drastic changes to the structure of major college athletics and because of the difficulty that many African American male student-athletes experience during their transition from high school to college, it is necessary to explore programs and services that help assist in the development of these individuals. Many universities and athletic departments have developed specific programs to address the general needs of student-athletes. For example, the NCAA's Student-Athlete Division provides numerous workshops that discuss key issues such as goal setting and action planning, leadership, service, and emotional intelligence for member universities (NCAA, 2014b). Universities have also created their own programs to address the particular academic and life skills that are critical to student-athletes' collegiate success. While these workshops have had some success, they tend to be overly general in order to reach all student-athletes, rather than African American males in particular. Thus, while the workshops can be of value, they often lack cultural relevance, or an ability to speak to a particular population in ways that are meaningful, empowering, and useful for that population (Ladson-Billings, 1995; Singer, 2005).

There is a great need to explore culturally relevant programming specifically directed towards African American male student-athletes, especially at predominantly White institutions (PWI) of higher learning. Ladson-Billings (1995) advocated for the need of such programming and perspectives within environments where there are major ethnic, racial, and cultural differences between faculty and administrators and the African American students and other ethnic minorities. African American male student-athletes have a unique burden of being a significant portion of the overall African American male population within the higher education system, while striving to succeed in a system that was originally not designed with their particular needs in mind (Engstrom, Sedlacek, & McEwen, 1995; Singer, 2005).

The purpose of this chapter is to provide insight into the transition and cultural integration of African American male student-athletes from high school to predominantly White NCAA Division I universities, based on the experiences of a group of African American male student-athletes at a large, public institution. In particular, the chapter will highlight the voice of the student-athletes to provide in-depth knowledge about the challenges they faced as they adjusted to the demands of a more competitive sports team, higher academic standards, and a new campus culture. This involved directly asking African American male student-athletes and key stakeholders to reflect on their own experiences and discuss their personal struggles, accomplishments, and behavioral changes during their first semesters at university.

LITERATURE REVIEW

Transition Theory

In the social sciences, researchers have taken interest in learning how individuals move through various phases and transitional points during their lifetimes. Defined as "any event, or non-event, that results in changed relationships, routines, assumptions, and roles" (Goodman, Schlossberg, & Anderson, 2006, p. 33), a transition can occur at any point in time for an individual and can be voluntary or involuntary, major or subtle, depending on the circumstance. There are different factors that can either ease or hinder one's transition into a new environment, as well as factors that help determine whether a transition was successful.

Nancy Schlossberg (1981) has been credited with developing a theory of transition that continues to influence a number of contexts, including higher education student development. In her seminal article "A Model for Analyzing Human Adaptation to Transition," Schlossberg made her key argument as to what influences a transition: "Ease of adaptation to a transition depends on one's perceived and/or actual balance of resources to deficits in terms of the transition itself, the pre-post environment, and the individual's sense of competency, well-being, and health" (Schlossberg, 1981, pp. 7-8).

Schlossberg and other scholars refined transition theory focusing more on a reaction to transition, rather than complete adaptation, since full adaptation to a transition is not always achieved (Evans, Forney, Guido, Patton, & Renn, 2010). Goodman, Schlossberg, & Anderson (2006) furthered the transition theoretical framework, providing more depth and details about transitions themselves and the major factors influencing those transitions. They posited that in order to understand transitions, one must consider the type of transition, the context, and the impact of the transition. Types of transitions include anticipated transitions, unanticipated transitions, and non-events or transitions that are expected and do not occur (Goodman et al., 2006). Meanwhile, context refers to the setting of the transition and an individual's relationship with the transition, whereas impact is the degree to which the transition changes one's life.

Goodman et al. (2006) also identified the four major sets of factors that influence a person's ability to deal with a transition: situation, self, social support, and strategies. Known commonly as the 4 Ss (Evans et al., 2010), an individual's resources (or lack thereof) in these areas help determine how effective the individual is at coping with the transition. The "situation" factors center on issues such as timing, control, role change, and duration of the transition among other variables. The "self" factors are demographic characteristics (e.g., race, gender, age, socioeconomic status, etc.) and psychological characteristics. The "social support" factors include relationships, family units, social networks, and institutions. Lastly, the "strategies" are types of coping factors, including behaviors that change the situation, control the meaning of the problem for the individual, and help manage and alleviate stress.

Emerging Adulthood: The Process of Becoming an Adult

As an adolescent turns 18 and begins to embark on new ambitions such as college (two- or four-year), the military, or other professional pathways, they enter a phase in their growth called *emerging adulthood*. This theory of transition describes a period of time that is distinct from the adolescence period, associated with the teenage years, and full adulthood, where these individuals are subject to enduring responsibilities that come with being an independent adult (Arnett, 2000). The period of emerging adulthood is "characterized by change and exploration for most people as they examine the life possibilities open to them and gradually arrive at more enduring choices in love, work, and worldviews" (Arnett, 2000, p. 479). Emerging adulthood is distinct and is evidenced in three ways: 1) demographics (e.g., residential status); 2) the subjective nature of the transition (individuals categorizing themselves as adults, adolescents, or neither); and 3) the chance to explore one's identity in relationships, professional life, and worldview. This developmental stage is critical and salient during the transition of individuals in industrialized nations from high school to college.

Transition from High School to College

One of the most common transitions for many individuals after they graduate high school is the transition to being a college student. The first year of college is often cited as the most critical year for college students in terms of retention, persistence, and potential to graduate (Chemers, Hu, & Garcia, 2001). Transitions into college can certainly vary by type, context, and impact as well. The 4 Ss certainly play a significant role in mitigating the challenges of this transition for individuals entering college. Academic preparation, socioeconomic status (SES), race, and gender among others have all been looked upon as factors that can help predict whether students will enroll, persist, and graduate from college (Cabrera, Nora, & Castañeda, 1992; Light & Strayer, 2002; Paulsen & John, 2002). Not only do new college students have to deal with the academic and social pressures of their transition, but they often must also face a transition into adulthood with an increased amount of autonomy compared to what they previously had at home (Bozick & DeLuca, 2005).

Student-Athlete Transition: Competing Identities and Culture

In addition to the challenges that all students face as they graduate high school and enter college, NCAA Division I student-athletes must deal with the transition from competitive, varsity high school sports, to high-pressure, elite intercollegiate athletics. In particular, the athletic adjustment can provide equal, if not greater challenges to the student's adjustment than academic and social adjustments. The sport development literature alludes to the difficulty in adjusting to new levels of elite sport. Green (2005) argued that "when an athlete moves to a more advanced team, club, or squad, the athlete must adjust to a new cohort of athletes, new coaching, and new expectations" (p. 247). Essentially the athlete has to deal with the conflict of having to be re-socialized into a sport that he or she has already been socialized into at lower levels in their past sport experiences.

The African American male student-athlete will not only have to deal with the dual role transition as student and athlete, but will also be confronted with other challenges, such as athletic identity racial stereotypes. Scholars have explored the relationship between athletic involvement, athletic participation, and athletic identity to academic and career development at both the secondary and postsecondary levels and have found evidence to support both arguments for and against athletic involvement having a positive impact on academic performance and career outcomes. Murphy, Petitpas, and Brewer (1996) shed light on the importance of the relationship between student-athletes' athletic identity foreclosure and how it negatively effects their career development. Brown, Glastetter-Fender, and Shelton's (2000) study on student-athletes' psychosocial identity and the control of their career decisions, found that the athletes' extensive participation in sports and their foreclosure within their sport identity was inversely related to their ability to make important career decisions that could influence their future careers outside of sports.

In addition to having a strong relationship with athletic identity, African American male student-athletes must also face stereotyping and racial prejudice. Harry Edwards (1984) brought forth the stereotypical term of the "Dumb Black Jock," who is a brute that is brought to the university to only play sports with no effort or expectation of his achieving educational success. Numerous researchers have demonstrated the existence and prevalence of this view in the higher education environment (Engstrom & Sedlacek, 1989; C. K. Harrison, 1998; Sailes, 1993; Singer, 2005, 2008). This notion has been shown to prevail even in the present day. Harrison, Sailes, Rotich, and Bimper's (2011) study showed the increased salience of the athletic identity to African American student-athletes and how they felt others perceived them only as athletes and not necessarily as student-athletes. Thus, not only do the attitudes amongst faculty and the campus community exist, but African American student-athletes are aware of how other people view them in both university and non-university settings.

METHODOLOGY

This study focused on the needs of African American male student-athletes, as they perceived them, during the transition from high school to college at historically predominantly White NCAA institutions. Thus, it largely centered on understanding the lived experiences of these athletes and how they perceived their lives, their needs, and their sources of support. Such study is the purview of constructionist epistemology and symbolic interactionism perspective, both of which try to understand the lived experiences of individuals in their social world and how they come to understand and interpret their world and the meaning of their experiences within it (Blumer, 1969; Burr, 2003).

Given the study's focus on developing in-depth descriptions from and about the participants, its flexibility, and the evolving nature in which data was collected, I utilized an inductive method for this study (Baker, Wuest, & Stern, 1992; Munhall, 2007). This method is also well suited to bring fresh insight and ideas to the project as it will allow for new developments and twists on the emerging theory (Charmaz, 2006). Yet, it can also supply rigor and structure to the qualitative process through its explicit procedures and strategies for collecting data and formulating theory (Charmaz, 2006).

Participant Recruitment

A total of 12 first-year African American male student-athletes were recruited to provide direct and relevant perspectives regarding their needs as African American male student-athletes transitioning from high school to a predominantly White institution of higher education. Additionally, four upperclassmen student-athletes and three former student-athletes, all African American, were recruited to participate in the study and provide additional depth to the findings. Other stakeholders such as faculty, staff, and athletic department personnel who worked closely with African American male student-athletes were also interviewed. All of the current and former student-athlete participants were scholarship football players for this institution. The study participants were recruited from a large, public flagship university in the Southwestern United States that participates at the Division I, Football Bowl Subdivision (FBS) level in the NCAA. This institution is also considered a historically predominantly White institution. Using my professional and social networks, participants were contacted and invited to participate in the study. A combination of snowball and theoretical sampling was used to identify additional participants. In the case of snowball sampling, participants were asked to provide names of potential participants to contact for future interviews. Upon learning of potential participants, theoretical sampling was utilized to help strategically select the best potential participants (Singer, 2005).

To ensure confidentiality during and after the research process, participants did not provide identifying information (e.g., addresses or any other sensitive information) during the interviews. Participants were reminded that the conversations were confidential and that they could choose to stop their participation at any time and refusal would not impact current or future relationships with the research lab used to conduct the study and/or the educational institution of the student-athletes. Data was de-identified and pseudonyms were used throughout the process.

STUDY DESIGN

Procedure

Potential participants were contacted in person, by telephone, or via email and invited to participate. Then, voluntary verbal consent was obtained, and arrangements were made to conduct the interview. Prior to the interview, each first-year student-athlete participant filled out a demographic questionnaire to capture detailed information describing the participant. Questions regarding the participants' race/ethnicity, socioeconomic status, standardized test scores, academic performance, and other pertinent details were included. The results of the questionnaire would be used to add further depth to the qualitative data gained through the interview and provide a profile of the student-athletes this study focused on. Interviews were conducted in a controlled, private space selected by either the participant or me and mutually agreed upon prior to the interview. Interviews were digitally recorded to ensure accuracy of what was said. The interviews lasted 45 minutes to 1.5 hours.

Instrument

A semi-structured interview format was utilized to collect data. This less formal interview format sought to gain a comprehensive description and better understanding of the participants' experience without imposing any researcher-bound notions or assumptions that would limit the inquiry (Creswell, 2002). Nonetheless, as opposed to loosely guided exploration interviews, these interviews were slightly focused (Charmaz, 2006). The interviews incorporated an objective approach in the beginning to get the participant to speak about his life, but then shifted into a more constructivist approach to gather the participants' thoughts on subject matter as they see it (Charmaz, 2006; Glaser, 1978; Strauss & Corbin, 1990). Thus, the interviews were more of a directed conversation that started with broad, general-experience-type questions, then narrowed to more specific probes based on the participants' responses. This aided in tapping into more latent concepts such as "needs" that may not have manifested themselves in direct lines of questioning (Doherty, Fink, Inglis, & Pastore, 2010; Lofland & Lofland, 1995).

Interview questions were developed from the college student development literature. The questions were reviewed for face validity by a panel of experts in qualitative research, race and culture studies, sport management, and student development before implementation. Additional probes—such as "Tell me more about that" and "Can you give me an example?"—were used to gather additional insight and follow up any particular question with more in-depth discussion.

Data Analysis

Upon completion of the interviews, the digital recordings were then professionally transcribed and analyzed with the aid of NVIVO 9 research software for analysis and insight into qualitative data. Using an open or initial coding process, the data were first coded line by line. The codes initially identified were then clustered into larger abstract categories called themes in a process called axial coding. This helped to sort, synthesize, and organize large amounts of data and reassemble them in new ways after open coding (Creswell, 1998). Theoretical coding was then utilized to not only help tell a story, but move the story in a theoretical direction by conceptualizing how codes are related (Charmaz, 2006). Through successive iterations and comparing within and between cases, intuitive ideas about the properties and relationships of the codes and themes were checked with the data until more concrete themes and related subthemes emerged (Munhall, 2007, p. 252).

The interviews with the subjects were conducted to help identify and bring out the aforementioned themes. Through these interviews, the demographic survey, and follow-up interviews, I was able to obtain rich data. The most representative quotes were selected to exemplify the emergent themes and categories that help to answer the proposed research questions of the study. To certify the accuracy of the codes and themes that emerged, and to provide for a check of authenticity, member checks were conducted (Munhall, 2007). More specifically, participants were able to read their transcripts and provide feedback regarding both the content of the transcripts and the interpretation of the coding and themes. To ensure confidentiality, all subject names were removed and replaced with pseudonyms that are used throughout this chapter.

RESULTS

The use of semi-structured interviews allowed for consistent questioning of the participants, yet created the flexibility for the participants to take the conversation in the directions they wanted and be frank and candid with the interviewer. During the interview process, while there was a set of questions for the interviewer to ask each of the participants, the participants were allowed to speak freely without interruption and be as candid as possible.

The first-year African American male student-athletes were either 18 or 19 years of age at the time of their interviews. Five of the participants were from suburban cities, while four participants were from urban cities, and three participants were from rural hometowns. Of the first-year participants, 11 out of the 12 were from high schools within the same state as the university. Nine out of the 11 first-year student-athletes from the in-state cities attended high schools with 2,065 or more students as confirmed by their state's interscholastic athletic competition classification (Associated Press, 2010). While all of the first-year student-athletes were undeclared at the time of their interviews, seven out of the 12 participants indicated that they intended to major in an area within the kinesiology, physical culture and sport, or sport management fields.

In regard to college readiness, the first-year student-athletes had a wide range of standardized test scores and came from high schools that typically had lower college readiness rankings. For the SAT Reasoning Test, the student-athletes had verbal scores ranging from 200-430 (mean: 375) and math scores ranging from 200-530 (mean: 410). For those student-athletes who took the ACT, the average total score for the test was 17. Only two out of the 12 student-athletes took an Advanced Placement (AP) course and/or exam during high school. Based on *The U.S. News and World Report* "Best High Schools Rankings," the average college readiness index for the high schools the student-athletes attended was 14.2 out of a possible score of 100 (Morse, 2012).

The participants typically graduated from majority minority high schools with socioeconomically diverse student bodies. According to the *U.S. News and World Report* "Best High School Rankings," the average minority enrollment at the participants' high schools was 70% and typically had an average of 30% African Americans attending the high school. One of the participant's schools had a minority enrollment of 100%, of which 98% of the students were African American. The mean percentage of students considered economically disadvantaged (% of students on free and reduced lunch) was 49% (Morse, 2012).

Comparatively, the student population of the university the student-athletes attended was quite different than that of their high schools. While the institution's total undergraduate enrollment was comprised of 49% minority students, African American students made up less than 5% of the undergraduate student population. Academic performance varied for the participants in the study. Reported GPA's at the end of the second semester fell in a range from 2.33 to 3.07. The mean GPA for the first-year participants was a 2.65—only slightly lower than the institution's average freshman GPA of 2.73.

The household statistics were also varied among the participants. Six of the 12 participants were first-generation college students, meaning that neither one of their biological parents graduated from college. Out of the other six participants who were not considered first-generation college students, only two came from households where both parents held bachelor's degrees. Nine of the 12 participants chose to answer the question regarding their household income. Out of the nine respondents, seven had a household income of less than $75,000—five of which had incomes of less than $50,000.

Athletically, the participants were some of the most talented and highly recruited high school football players in their state and the nation as well. All of them were ranked by major online recruiting services such as Rivals, ESPNU, and Scout. According to the Rivals rankings, the participants had an average national position ranking of 20 and an overall average state ranking of 32. As for the ESPNU rankings, the average position ranking was 22, while the overall average state ranking was 41. Based on the Scout rankings, the average position ranking for the participants was 18 and the average overall state ranking was 37. Thus, these student-athletes were, on average, one of the top 25 rated players at their position in the nation and one of the top 50 players overall in their state. Based on these rankings, multiple top football programs from across the nation would likely have been happy to have these talented players attend their universities.

Three major themes emerged from the interviews: 1) Football is the hardest class on campus: A sense of feeling overwhelmed with their academic and athletic responsibilities; 2) The de-recruitment process: Being a high-profile student-athlete feels like being a business employee; 3) Stereotypes of a Black male (athlete) misunderstood: Encountering differential treatment due to their status as an African American male student-athlete. Out of these three themes, the third one seemed to permeate their entire student-athlete academic experience. These African American male student-athletes felt they were perceived and treated differently by various members of a predominantly White institution because of their status as high-profile, African American male student-athletes. The following sections will highlight this unique experience of being treated differently as a Black male student-athlete primarily using the words and thoughts of the 12 African American first-year males and key stakeholders interviewed.

The Differential Treatment of African American Male Student-Athletes on Campus

Throughout the conversation with the participants, the topic of racism came up often and usually was discussed at length. The history and culture of the predominantly White university created a sense of Whiteness that permeated the campus and which came as a culture shock to the African American male student-athletes. The most common issue brought up throughout the entire study centered on the negative stereotyping of African American male student-athletes and African American football players in particular. Every participant, including the upperclassmen, faculty, and staff members, agreed that African American football players were negatively stereotyped, often resulting in differential treatment from various groups of people all across the college campus. The participants also brought up issues regarding racism and its existence on campus and in the surrounding community. The participants' reflections can be divided into five major subcategories: the culture shock of being on a predominantly White campus, the most prevalent stereotypes of African American male student-athletes, differential treatment from academic staff, differential treatment from professors, and differential treatment from other students.

The Shock of Being Immersed into a Dominant White Culture on Campus

This large, predominantly White institution of higher learning often provided a sense of culture shock for a lot of the participants upon arrival due to not only the large amount of White students, but also the dominant White culture and the lack of other African American students on campus. The university they attended had a history of perceived elitism, racial segregation, and racism on campus. Clint, who's worked on campus for over 10 years, described the history. "This one [institution] in particular has a history of being not predominantly White, but being exclusively White," he said. "And as much as we'd like to think that history has changed, that history isn't that old." Deborah, who's worked at the university since the 1980s, confirmed that the history in fact was not that old and described racial incidents that took place as recently as the 1990s and 2000s.

In addition to the history of racism and the pervasive White culture at the institution, the large percentage of White students at the university was a shock to many of the participants from African American or diverse communities. Shawn described his experience as overwhelming at first. "I came from my hometown and when I was there, the makeup was about 50-50 [African American and White]," he explained. "Coming to a university of this size, you know there's fifty thousand and just the few number of African Americans—it overwhelms you." Alvin described his initial feelings as "weird." He expounded, "It's just a lot of White people. Just a lot of White people man. I don't know. Like as a Black guy you always hear 'Don't talk to any Whites.'" Patrick also added, "I didn't take this into account during my recruiting process, but I don't see how I fit in. Like my high school was all Black and all I know is Black people. I get here and it's all like [White]."

Phillip was highly concerned about attending a predominantly White school during his recruitment:

> I didn't like that. That's one reason why I really didn't want to come here. I was like, "Man! I can't be around these White folks." Like it ain't my type of environment. But my coach was talking to me and told me, "You've got to be able to change yourself sometimes and not be all in the hood and stuff because you're trying to get your mom out of that environment." Which is true, but I don't know. I'm just kind of worried because I didn't know what they're saying, all these kind of White folks.

Phillip not only highlighted a concern about not fitting into the culture at the university, but also an initial mistrust of White people based on his experience—a feeling that Nate echoed in his interview: "Especially being at a White university, it's tougher for us to trust a lot of the White folks around here."

While most examples of feeling culture shock came from participants from predominantly African American neighborhoods, some participants who came from predominantly White communities also felt overwhelmed at times. Randall, who was from a middle-class, White, suburban town, described an experience of how he felt unwanted in certain social settings:

> Yeah, because in my hometown, even though it's predominantly White, I mostly kind of knew the kids from seventh grade. So I had a small group of friends that I hung out with, and they knew me. But, I guess, when I got here, like if you try to, like freshman year, you can't go downtown or anything. So, if you try to go to one of these frat houses, like they won't tell you straight out, "Hey, we don't like Black people here," but they let it [be] known that, "Hey, we don't like Black people here." And so that kind of made me think that when you walk in, they will be cool. They will think it's cool at first, if there's one or two [Black athletes]. But the moment a White girl comes up and tries to start talking to you, they will try to walk them away and tell them, "No, no, no, you don't want to talk to him." Or, "He's

just a dumb athlete." And you can hear them say stuff like that, and you kind of get the feeling that, "Oh, they don't want you here." Or, they will see you in school, and say, "Hey, come to our party." But then when you get to the door, they will meet you at the door, and say, "Oh, you know, we don't want any athletes in here." You know, and stuff like that. It's just different.

While many of the participants learned how to mitigate or deal with the circumstances of being one of the few African Americans in many of their on-campus settings, occasionally some participants still struggled to adjust. Some of the participants were able to feel comfortable, or find safe spaces, within the White campus. Greg discussed these safe places in more detail and argued that, in some instances and spaces, their experience was better than other African American students:

> When you go to the academic center, Black males are the majority. That's amazing to me, because when I go to work every day, I see nothing but brothers [African American men], in an upscale academic area. So, you know, it's almost like they're the majority in their world. And in the weight room, in the academic room, on the field, and how they celebrate it in a majority White school, and what they see day to day is astonishing. And if they're going to an AFR [African American Studies] class, they're going to see more African Americans. I think their experience, from a Black perspective, is probably a little bit better. And like I said, the main picture, you've got to paint it at that academic center, majority Blacks—Black males only and a few of the White students. But they dominate the academic center area. That's who we see in all the rooms mostly.

On the other hand, some African American male student-athletes, like Patrick, still struggled with the culture shock despite being on campus for close to two years. As Patrick explained:

> I gotta adjust to the culture shock; this place is different from my city. It's just being around people you're not familiar with; it's hard to determine who has got your best interests or who to trust. I don't know how to overcome that. I really don't.

The culture shock of being on a predominantly White campus was a significant challenge for many of these African American male student-athletes. Whether they came from predominantly Black, racially mixed, or predominantly White communities, the lack of diversity on campus simply made them feel overwhelmed and often isolated as African American males. This finding affirmed Hyatt's (2003) argument of the lack of integration and isolation being a barrier for African American male student-athletes in the effort to persist at predominantly White institutions. The campus environment at this particular predominantly White institution also proved to be fertile for the use and belief in stereotypes of African American male student-athletes amongst members of the campus community.

Most Prevalent Stereotypes of African American Male Student-Athletes

While the literature has documented numerous, negative stereotypes regarding African American males and African American male athletes, there were some stereotypes that were more commonly referred to in this study (see Table 1 for a detailed list). The stereotype most often cited by all the participants was the "dumb Black jock" stereotype. Not only was this the most cited stereotype, but it also arguably had the most impact on the student-athletes' experiences with others. When asked if African American male student-athletes are stereotyped, the answers ranged from statements as short as "he's dumb" to longer and detailed experiences about being personally perceived as a dumb Black athlete. Lawrence talked about the dumb Black jock stereotype at length:

> Oh yeah…you [are] dumb. Don't get me wrong—you are dumb unless you can prove it. Otherwise they just know you're trying to make it; hoping that the Black athlete plays all four years and gets to the league before failing out because he isn't gonna graduate.

In terms of how others begin to view you because of this stereotype, Randall said, "They really don't expect much of you."

Other stereotypes of African American male student-athletes included sentiments regarding the value of the academic experience, negative perceptions of work ethic, and relationships with females, among others. For instance, some of the participants lamented that people see them as not valuing their education and only being here for football. Some of the participants also knew that they were stereotyped as being lazy and not having to work hard as other students because they're pampered athletes.

Table 1: Stereotypes of African American Male Student-Athletes

Stereotype	Representative Quote
They're automatically assumed to be an athlete.	"You know, and so, I mean, I always have those people. 'Oh, you know, what sport did you play?' They don't even actually ask you what sport… it jumps from asking do you play sports, to what sport you do play?" (Chris)
They always get into trouble.	"We're always downtown doing stupid stuff." (Randall)
They're babied or pampered.	"So, there are stereotypes within the Black community, that you know, the athletes are babied and given so many privileges." (Greg)

Stereotype	Representative Quote
They don't care about academics.	"All we are about is playing sports; we really don't care about academics." (Rob)
They're only here to play sports.	"I mean, of course you're not here for an education." (Chris)
They're sex crazed, here to sleep with multiple women.	"We're here to get girls." (Rob)
They're only interested in White women.	"You talk to White girls they [Black girls] ain't gonna talk to you, man. But it's funny, man. That's a huge stereotype." (Alvin)
They always take the easy way out.	"You know, that a lot of people expect us to take the easy route, the easy way out." (Chris)
They're natural athletes and don't work hard.	"They see us as already having talent and not having to work for anything." (Maurice)
They're not appreciative of their opportunity.	"People think that I'm not grateful." (Maurice)
They don't use their brain in sports.	"'Cause it's always, you know, some of the sports, it ain't nothing about our brains" (Phillip)
They don't deserve to be here.	"Those guys are only here for football; they don't deserve to be here." (Nate)
They're dumb.	"We're dumb. Like we're really just not up to par when it comes to the classroom and getting the grades." (Rob)

Additionally, they also lamented the stereotypes that they really only cared about sleeping with women and being typecast by their African American female peers as only interested in White women.

While the stereotypes of African American male student-athletes tended to be mainly negative, the stereotypes of White male student-athletes tended to be more positive. In direct opposition to the dumb Black jock stereotype, White student-athletes were stereotyped as good students academically. Clint talked about how coaches were surprised that some of their White student-athletes were not doing well in school because they had bought into this stereotype:

> I have coaches ask me, "How can so and so do so badly last semester?" And I'm like, "Because he's a dumb ass. Have you not talked to him?" Oh I get it, he's a White kid, and his parents come down to all the games, so we automatically assume he's a better student than he is, because he doesn't fit your profile.

The participants not only knew of the White athletes' stereotypes compared to their own, but often they felt as if they received differential treatment from the athletic department's academic staff, professors, and their peers. This is very consistent with the current research regarding stereotypes of African American male student-athletes completed in the past and more recently, confirming how pervasive and entrenched these stereotypes are in American culture (Benson, 2000; Edwards, 1984; Singer, 2005).

Differential Treatment From Professors

Another way that stereotypes affect African American male student-athletes' experience is with their interactions and relationships with professors. Professors are not immune to buying into stereotypes. The participants in the study actually reflected numerous times on experiences where they felt professors, especially White professors, labeled them or judged them based on their status as a scholarship athlete. Clint explained the differential treatment of White student-athletes versus African American male student-athletes.

> The initial meeting with a White football player and a faculty member may be where a faculty member assumes that they're a better student than they are, 'cause they look like all the other students, again in their minds. Whereas, the African American football student-athlete will meet with a faculty member, and they will assume that they're only here because they're not a great talented student, but they're a much more talented athlete.

Based upon this observation and input from the participants, it seemed that the participants perceived that professors made snap judgments about the intellectual capabilities of African American male student-athletes based on the common stereotype of not caring about education. This stereotype also became an issue for professors worried about how they were perceived by their peers or faculty members from other departments when they had many African American male student-athletes in their classes. Clint added:

> I've had faculty members ask me why they had so many African American football players in their class. Well, it's because it's [at] 10 o'clock in the morning, and they have to be out

of class at 1 [PM], and it's a requirement for everybody on this campus...So we are going to have certain segments of our student-athlete population in courses that are available at particular times that meet particular requirements, not necessarily because of who the instructor is...But this particular faculty member was concerned because he had peers in his department ask him, "Why?" And his fear was that he would be considered a jock sniffer by his peers, and therefore, was hooking up athletes with grades they hadn't earned.

Fred also gave an example of how professors are constantly questioning the integrity of his work:

There was this time when I had done my work, and it was some good work and [they'll ask] "Did you do this all by yourself?" Some people don't think it's that big of a deal. But to me, I mean, I'm a normal kid just like everybody else. I can do my work...But it's happened multiple times...People assuming that just because I'm an African American male, that I just need help with every single thing.

Some of the student-athletes were also shocked to find professors did not care about how you performed in the class. Nate explained this concept:

I feel like with us, with the Black student-athletes...we need the professors that actually care about us, you know. We don't need the professor that just doesn't care if anyone in the class fails. We need guys that are actually going to teach us and also want us to learn.

The participants wanted professors who cared and taught well, as this would motivate and inspire them to learn.

The participants also felt that they could talk to Black professors, as opposed to White professors. Lawrence explained how he felt about speaking with White professors:

It was easier for me to talk to Black professors than White. But I learned to get over that, but I couldn't talk to White professors at first. I really couldn't talk to White professors. I felt like if I talked to them they were going to go back and tell somebody that this kid isn't what he was; this kid's not that student they said he was. So, I never really told anybody that like I couldn't talk to White professors. I still somewhat feel like I can't talk to them, but I go and do it anyway because sometimes you gotta stick your neck out there. But you're uncomfortable sometimes.

Like Lawrence, many of the participants were able to get over some of their initial fears of professors and White professors in particular. For instance, Randall decided to not worry about what the professors thought, and just "let the work prove itself," while other African American male student-athletes just quietly did their work and went about their business without interacting much with the professors. This finding may affirm past research demonstrating African American male student-athletes' hesitation to interact with White professors (Comeaux & Harrison, 2007; Perlmutter, 2003).

Differential Treatment From Other Students

Stereotypes of African American male student-athletes really seemed to be most pervasive among other non-athlete students on campus. The "dumb Black jock" that does not care about his education was perceived to be the most commonly held stereotype among students and often it played a major role in classroom dynamics. When students were split up into group projects, the students who were assigned to groups with an African American male student-athlete often warned him to take the work seriously or would push him to the side while they did the rest of the work so that he could focus on football and not bring down their grade. Alvin expounded:

> You have a group project. Sometimes they don't give you anything to do on the project. They're just "Oh, we'll take care of everything." One, they may not think you're capable; two, they just want to do it anyways 'cause you're an athlete.

Everett also mentioned that he often gets offers to do his work or help him out with classes so that he can perform on game day:

> I go into a class at the beginning of the semester and two weeks later, somebody will write me a message on Facebook saying "Hey man, I see that you're in this class. If you need any help, just hit me up. I gotcha my man. I just want you to do well on the field." So, I mean, the stereotype is that we're just here for sports and that's it.

Randall provided an example of treatment he received from students in class who assumed he was just an athlete and contrasted that with the experience of one of his White teammates:

> I've had people just come up to me and say, "Don't worry. I will do this work, and you can just copy it." I'm like, "No, man. I can do the work. It's not like that." They don't really expect much out of you. And, I mean, that's the stereotyping, or racism. But then I've been in classes with my White teammates, and they're not looked at the same way. They're expected to be smart and able to do the work. And people don't come up to them and ask them, "Hey, what do you do?"

Thus, looking at the experiences of African American male student-athletes on campus, it is evident that race, racism, and stereotypes play a major role in how others perceived them and how they are treated on a regular basis. Though people may or may not explicitly view them through the lens of race, African American male student-athletes are reminded frequently that their race and their status as an athlete does matter on and around campus.

DISCUSSION

While the overall transition from high school to college in terms of athletics and academics were expected, some of the other transitions they went through were unexpected and may have surprised them or impacted their transition greater than the transitions they did expect. Looking back at Schlossberg's (1981) theory of transition, an individual's ability to transition and potential to adapt to it depends greatly on the individual's perception of the transition, their personal characteristics, and the characteristics of their old and new environment. Perhaps the biggest issue for many of the participants in this study was the stark contrast of the characteristics of their old environment compared to their new environment on campus. Since their old environment was much more diverse racially compared to their new environment, it made transitioning to a predominantly White institution—with a history of a powerful and dominant upper-middle class White culture—that much more difficult for the participants. Additionally, their old environments provided much more comfort and support because of the existence of strong and loving families compared to a campus that not only created a physical barrier between their life at school and home, but also forced these young men to encounter a sometimes hostile environment on their own.

Goodman et al.'s (2006) argument that transitions are understood by considering the type, context, and impact of transition also revealed a lot about the transitions that African American male student-athletes endure during their first year. The type of transition was arguably the biggest issue and also had the most impact for this population, followed by the context and impact.

The transition from a more diverse community to an environment that is a significantly less diverse and dominated by upper-middle class, White cultural norms proved to be the transition that left a great impression on this group of Black male student-athletes. This transition was largely unanticipated by the student-athletes, despite knowing upfront that they were attending a predominantly White institution. Nonetheless, the sheer number of students and the minimal number of students who looked like them, made these young men stand out even more in the majority of places on campus. This resulted in African American male student-athletes often experiencing culture shock, feeling out of place, or perceiving that they were being judged by the negative stereotypical assumptions associated with African American male athletes. The context speaks for itself in this situation, as many of the young men had to grow accustomed to being in an environment where they were outnumbered and where the power dynamics of race also became an issue when working with academic staff, professors, and even their coaches. Lastly, the impact of the transition was major as the participants were now required to adjust to new cultural norms and were confronted with racial stereotypes throughout the rest of their experience on campus.

This study's findings imply that race is a significant factor in the transitional experiences of male student-athletes at a predominantly White institution. While there are issues that are salient regardless of race, there are some issues that are impacted by it. Clearly, issues related to the pervasive negative stereotypes of African

American male student-athletes affected them in their athletic, academic, and psychosocial settings. The issues surrounding race did not have the same impact on Anglo-American student-athletes, due in part to the fact that they were able to blend into the university environment more easily than African American male student-athletes.

Implications for Higher Education

The study yielded multiple important implications for institutions of postsecondary education that are interested in improving the transition from high school to college for African American male student-athletes. These implications include the need to: 1) create mentoring programs for African American male student-athletes that incorporate African American male professors, staff, and professionals from the community, among others; 2) foster connections between African American male student-athletes and African American male students; 3) provide diversity and cultural sensitivity training for coaches and athletic staff employees; 4) support the creation of small academic communities within their sport that create a competitive culture of academic success; 5) inform African American male student-athletes where they can find additional psychological and psychosocial support (general and culturally specific), both on and off campus.

This investigation confirms the need for connections to a larger community than merely the other African American male student-athletes on their team. The participants often felt that they could only relate to other African American male student-athletes due to the fact that other non-athletes couldn't relate to them. Part of the problem stems from the isolation that many of these young men operate in because of the demands of their sport and the amount of time they spend in their sports facilities. Participants spoke of the value they received from spending time with professors like Dr. Voorhees, who provided mentoring sessions and introduced them to people and concepts they may have never known. A mentoring program for African American male student-athletes that incorporates African American male faculty and staff and professionals from the community could foster a connection to real examples of African American males who are successful in various fields outside of athletics. Additionally, this same medium could be used to integrate African American male students and help build relationships and expand the community they consider themselves a part of. This type of connection would also be helpful to eliminate some of the stereotypes that the general African American male students have of African American male student-athletes and vice versa.

This investigation also affirms the need for a stronger relationship between the academic departments and athletic department. The staff members from athletics mentioned that they had good relationships with some professors on campus and often feel comfortable directing their student-athletes to take courses with these professors. With the tensions that exist between athletic and academic departments due to money and funding issues and philosophical differences on the true purpose of higher education, it is imperative for athletic departments to reach out to faculty and academic departments across the university. Athletic departments should also partner with diversity units on campus to promote diversity education for all faculty and staff that may help breakdown the negative stereotypes and promote better understanding of African American male student-athletes. A good relationship with faculty could lead to potentially creating more course and major opportunities for student-athletes and potentially more faculty who are supportive of student-athletes attending the university.

Athletic departments should also continue to recruit and retain qualified and high-caliber African American talent on their academic and support services staffs. These individuals are often responsible for interacting with student-athletes and preparing training and orientations for them as they enter the university. It is critical that there is a staff that is diverse in terms of gender, race, and backgrounds. This is helpful when it comes to designing materials and events for student-athletes with diverse identities in mind. In particular for this group, it is essential to have African American males represented in different areas of the athletic staff, from high-level staff down to the hourly staff workers like tutors and mentors.

Athletic departments should also make an effort to connect with African American alumni from major metropolitan areas within their state and also make an effort to invite them to many of the athletic department events held with alumni and donors. This will provide a network of African American professionals that can be leveraged for a mentoring program for African American male student-athletes, as well as for speaking engagements and other opportunities. Additionally, some of the participants mentioned how out of place they felt at some of the events they attended with major donors and friends of the program that consisted mainly of Anglo-American men. The participants said that they often did not feel very comfortable speaking with these individuals and sometimes felt their interest in the student-athletes was not genuine. Therefore, having a more diverse audience at these events may make them seem less daunting for some African American male student-athletes to attend.

REFERENCES

Arnett, J. J. (2000). A theory of development from the late teens through the twenties. *American Psychologist*, 55(5), 469–480.

Associated Press. (2010). UIL district-by-district realignment changes. *ABC13.com*. Retrieved from http://abclocal.go.com/ktrk/story?section=news/sports&id=7251120

Baker, C., Wuest, J., & Stern, P. N. (1992). Method slurring: The grounded theory/phenomenology example. *Journal of Advanced Nursing, 17*(11), 1355–1360.

Benson, K. F. (2000). Constructing Academic Inadequacy. *Journal of Higher Education, 71*(2), 223–246.

Blumer, H. (1969). *Symbolic interactionism: Perspective and method.* Englewood Cliffs, NJ: Prentice-Hall.

Bozick, R., & DeLuca, S. (2005). Better late than never? Delayed enrollment in the high school to college transition. *Social Forces, 84*(1), 531–554.

Brown, C., Glastetter-Fender, C., & Shelton, M. (2000). Psychosocial identity and career control in college student-athletes. *Journal of Vocational Behavior, 56*, 53–62.

Burr, V. (2003). *Social constructionism* (2nd ed.). London, UK: Routledge.

Cabrera, A. F., Nora, A., & Castañeda, M. B. (1992). The role of finances in the persistence process: A structural model. *Research in Higher Education, 33*(5), 571–593.

Carter, P. L., & Welner, K. G. (Eds.). (2013). *Closing the opportunity gap: What America must do to give every child an even chance.* New York: Oxford University Press.

Charmaz, K. (2006). *Constructing grounded theory: A practical guide through qualitative analysis.* Thousand Oaks, CA: Sage.

Chemers, M. M., Hu, L., & Garcia, B. F. (2001). Academic self-efficacy and first-year college student performance and adjustment. *Journal of Educational Psychology, 93*(1), 55–64.

College Board. (2011). *2010 college-bound seniors: Total group profile report.* New York, NY: The College Board.

Comeaux, E., & Harrison, C. K. (2007). Faculty and male student athletes: Racial differences in the environmental predictors of academic achievement. *Race Ethnicity and Education, 10*(2), 199–214.

Creswell, J. W. (1998). *Qualitative inquiry and research design: Choosing among five traditions.* Thousand Oaks, CA: Sage.

Creswell, J. W. (2002). *Educational research: Planning, conducting, and evaluating quantitative and qualitative research.* Upper Saddle River, NJ: Pearson Education.

Doherty, A., Fink, J., Inglis, S., & Pastore, D. (2010). Understanding a culture of diversity through frameworks of power and change. *Sport Management Review, 13*, 368–381.

Donnor, J. (2005). Towards an interest-convergence in the education of African-American football student athletes in major college sports. *Race, Ethnicity & Education, 8*(1), 45–67.

Edwards, H. (1984). The Black "dumb jock": An American sports tragedy. *College Board Review, 131*, 8–13.

Eitzen, D. S. (2001). Big-time college sports: Contradictions, crises, and consequences. In D. S. Eitzen (Ed.), *Sport in contemporary society: An anthology* (pp. 201-212). New York: Worth.

Eitzen, D. S. (2009). The contradictions of big-time college sports. In D. S. Eitzen (Ed.), *Fair and foul: Beyond the myths and paradoxes of sport* (4th ed., pp. 165-204). Lanham, MD: Rowman & Littlefield Publishers.

Eitzen, D. S., & Purdy, D. A. (1986). The academic preparation and achievement of Black and White collegiate athletes. *Journal of Sport and Social Issues, 10*(1), 15–29.

Engstrom, C. M., & Sedlacek, W. E. (1989). *Attitudes of residence hall students toward student-athletes: Implications for advising, training, and programming.* College Park, MD: University of Maryland College Park Counseling Center.

Engstrom, C. M., Sedlacek, W. E., & McEwen, M. K. (1995). Faculty attitudes toward male revenue and nonrevenue student-athletes. *Journal of College Student Development, 36*(3), 217–227.

Evans, N. J., Forney, D. S., Guido, F. M., Patton, L. D., & Renn, K. A. (Eds.). (2010). *Student development in college: Theory, research, and practice* (2nd ed.). San Francisco: Jossey-Bass.

Glaser, B. G. (1978). *Theoretical sensitivity.* Mill Valley, CA: The Sociology Press.

Goodman, J., Schlossberg, N. K., & Anderson, M. L. (Eds.). (2006). *Counseling adults in transition: Linking practice with theory* (3rd ed.). New York, NY: Springer.

Green, B. C. (2005). Building sport programs to optimize athlete recruitment, retention, and transition: Toward a normative theory of sport development. *Journal of Sport Management, 19,* 233–253.

Harrison, C. K. (1998). Themes that thread through society: Racism and athletic manifestation in the African-American community. *Race Ethnicity and Education, 1*(1), 63–74.

Harrison, L., Harrison, C. K., & Moore, L. N. (2002). African American racial identity and sport. *Sport, Education and Society, 7*(2), 121–133.

Harrison, L., Sailes, G., Rotich, W. K., & Bimper, A. Y. (2011). Living the dream or awakening from the nightmare: Race and athletic identity. *Race Ethnicity and Education, 14,* 91–103.

Hawkins, B. (2001). *The new plantation: The internal colonization of Black student athletes.* Winterville, GA: Sadiki Press.

Hodge, S. R., Burden, J. W., Robinson, L. E., & Bennett III, R. A. (2008). Theorizing on the stereotyping of Black male student-athletes. *Journal for the Study of Sports and Athletes in Education, 2*(2), 203–226.

Hyatt, R. (2003). Barriers to persistence among African American intercollegiate athletes: A literature review of non-cognitive variables. *College Student Journal, 37*(2), 260.

Ladson-Billings, G. (1995). Toward a theory of culturally relevant pedagogy. *American Educational Research Journal, 32*(3), 465–491.

Light, A., & Strayer, W. (2002). From *Bakke* to *Hopwood*: Does race affect college attendance and completion? *The Review of Economics and Statistics, 84*(1), 34–44.

Lofland, J., & Lofland, L. H. (1995). *Analyzing social settings* (3rd ed.). Belmont, CA: Wadsworth.

Morse, R. (2012). Best High Schools Methodology. *U.S. News and World Report.* Retrieved from http://www.usnews.com/education/high-schools/articles/2012/05/07/best-high-schools-methodology?page=2

Munhall, P. L. (2007). *Nursing research : A qualitative perspective* (4th ed.). Sudbury, MA.: Jones and Bartlett.

Murphy, G. M., Petitpas, A. J., & Brewer, B. W. (1996). Identity foreclosure, athletic identity, and career maturity in intercollegiate athletes. *The Sport Psychologist, 10,* 239–246.

NCAA. (2014a). Aggregate Federal Graduation Rate Data Reports - Division I. Retrieved December 16, 2014, from http://www.ncaa.org/sites/default/files/2014-d1-grad-rate-aggregate.pdf

NCAA. (2014b). Leadership Development: Programs and Resources. Retrieved December 16, 2014, from http://www.ncaa.org/about/resources/leadership-development-programs-and-resources

Patterson, C. M. (2000). Athletics and the higher education marketplace. In J. R. Gerdy (Ed.), *Sports in school: The future of an institution* (pp. 119–127). New York, NY: Teachers College Press.

Paulsen, M. B., & John, E. P. S. (2002). Social class and college costs: Examining the financial nexus between college choice and persistence. *The Journal of Higher Education, 73*(2), 189–236.

Perlmutter, D. D. (2003). Black athletes and White professors: A twilight zone of uncertainty. *Chronicle of Higher Education, 50,* B7.

Person, D. R., Benson-Quaziena, M., & Rogers, A. M. (2001). Female student athletes and student athletes of color. *New Directions for Student Services, 2001*(93), 55–64.

Sailes, G. A. (1986). Guest Editorial: The exploitation of the Black athlete: Some alternative solutions. *The Journal of Negro Education, 55*(4), 439–442.

Sailes, G. A. (1993). An investigation of campus stereotypes: The myth of Black athletic superiority and dumb jock stereotypes. *Sociology of Sport Journal, 10,* 88–97.

Schlossberg, N. K. (1981). A model for analyzing human adaptation to transition. *The Counseling Psychologist, 9*(2), 2–18.

Singer, J. N. (2005). Understanding racism through the eyes of African American male student athletes. *Race, Ethnicity and Education, 8,* 365–386.

Singer, J. N. (2008). Benefits and detriments of African American male athletes' participation in a big-time college football program. *International Review for the Sociology of Sport, 43*(4), 399–408.

Steele, C. (1997). A threat in the air: How stereotypes shape intellectual identity and performance. *American Psychologist, 52,* 613–629.

Strauss, A., & Corbin, J. (1990). *Basics of qualitative research: Grounded theory procedures and techniques.* Newbury Park, CA: Sage.

CHAPTER FOUR

Brothers Gonna Work It Out: Black Male Academics Negotiating Mentorship, Fatherhood, and Partnerhood in a Community Context

RICHARD J. REDDICK AND JAMES THOMAS

How might one assess the status of the Black male in America in the year 2014? In many arenas, there is a considerable amount of good news to convey. For six years, the chief executive of the United States has been a Black man, Barack H. Obama. Performers such as Jay-Z, Tyler Perry, and Forest Whitaker dominate the world of entertainment. On many statistical indexes of educational attainment, we can see increases in high school diplomas or equivalents, bachelor's degrees, and master's and higher degrees (U.S. Census and U.S. Bureau of Labor Statistics, 2013). On the other hand, vivid examples of social inequities exist. One of 2013's most critically acclaimed films, *Fruitvale Station* (Whitaker, Bongiovi, & Coogler, 2014), chronicles the last day of 22-year-old Oscar Grant, murdered by police officers at a train station. The nation is still reeling from the aftermath of the shooting of 17-year-old Trayvon Martin at the hands of George Zimmerman, who was acquitted of murder despite shooting an unarmed teenager who was simply walking home from a convenience store (Robertson & Schwartz, 2012). Tragically, yet perhaps unsurprisingly, another case of an unarmed Black youth's death at the hands of a White police officer—18-year-old Michael Brown in Ferguson, Missouri—at the time of this writing, presently occupies the news cycle (Reddick & Vincent, 2014).

Recently, another high-achieving, college-aspiring young Black male, Jordan Davis, was labelled a "thug" when a fearful White man unilaterally decided that a loud car radio was deserving of death—what Obama's spiritual advisor Joshua DuBois (2014) terms as a "a foolish, lethal fear of Black teens" from Emmett Till in 1955 to Trayvon Martin and Jordan Davis in the 2010s. As fathers, uncles, mentors, and former Black boys, we wonder how far have we truly come in an alleged "postracial" society. The senior author reflects on having to have the same conversation with his son that his father had with him thirty-odd years ago—what every Black man refers to as "the talk" (Amber, 2013). Not about sex or drugs, but how to comport oneself when dealing with police and other vestiges of racist, patriarchal control—remain calm, comply with their directions, and note badge numbers and license plates—so you can live to see another day.

Aside from being fans of Public Enemy, there's a reason why Chuck D's lyric is the title of this chapter. We intend to discuss how Black men in academia negotiate their roles as partners, fathers (and father figures), mentors, and leaders in multiple community contexts. Despite media portrayals to the contrary, we believe that the Black community exalts men of faith and educators as leaders. These multiple roles often lead Black men to "over perform," leading to a phenomenon called "John Henryism," which can lead to deleterious health outcomes (James, Hartnett, & Kalsbeek, 1983). Through narrative, we will recall interactions and discussions with Black male scholars that point to this stress, with an ultimate goal to provoke discussion regarding how Black men in an exalted position share similar experiences. This is a chronicle of how "brothers work it out."

> (We're gonna do a song) that you never heard before
>
> Make you all jump along to the education brothers gonna work it out (Shocklee, Sadler, & Ridenhour, 1990)

LITERATURE REVIEW

There has been a steady increase in the participation of Black Americans in higher education for over half a century. Since the start of integration in the late 1950s and 1960s at predominantly White institutions (PWIs), the number of Blacks at these institutions has followed an upward trajectory. Along with this increase, Black scholars have increased their presence at PWIs, both in raw numbers and in representation among the senior faculty (American Council on Education, 2005; Tuitt, Hanna, Martinez, del Carmen Salazar, & Griffin, 2009). These generally positive indicators are mitigated by some troubling factors, however. A persistent gap exists between White and Asian completion rates at PWIs compared to those of Black students (Astin & Oseguera, 2005; Haycock, Lynch, & Engle, 2010). Additionally, the literature on the experiences of Black faculty and students at PWIs points to prejudice, racism, and isolation from the campus and community (Griffin & Reddick, 2011; Solórzano, Ceja, & Yosso, 2000; Thompson & Louque, 2005).

Allen, Epps, Guillory, Suh, and Bonous-Hammarth's (2000) examination of the status of Black faculty revealed that Black males spent more time weekly outside of class working with students, were more likely to spend more time providing academic counseling outside of class, and spent more time on administrative and committee work than White men. In the classroom, Black men confront challenges: Harlow (2003) found that Black men noted that students resisted their intellectual authority (i.e., knowledge and competency) more than Black women and White men and women, a finding corroborated by Hendrix (1998). Predominantly White classrooms are also danger zones for Black male professors; Jackson and Crawley (2003) found that "shocked and scared" were words used by White students to describe their initial impressions of a Black male faculty member. Smith (2004) has termed this pressure "racial battle fatigue," defined by the statement of a Black male professor:

> If you can think of the mind as having 100 ergs of energy, and the average man uses 50 percent of this energy dealing with the everyday problems of the world—just general kinds of things— then he has 50 percent more to do creative things that he wants to do. Now, that's a White person. Now, a Black person also has 100 ergs. He uses 50 percent the same way a White man does, dealing with what the White man has [to deal with], so he has 50 percent left. But he uses 25 percent fighting being Black [with] all the problems being Black and what it means. (As quoted in Smith, 2004, p. 171)

Racial battle fatigue is not isolated to campus experiences. Noted Black intellectual and Harvard professor Henry Louis "Skip" Gates made headlines in 2009 when he was arrested in front of his own home. The fact that someone who had scaled the summit of academia could be handcuffed and placed in jail for "disorderly conduct" for simply speaking to a police officer disrupted the idea that educational achievement could inoculate Black men from the ravages of racial inequity. As Yale professor Stephen Carter opined, "If it can happen to [Gates], possibly the most prominent black scholar in the country… then it can indeed happen to any of us" (as quoted in Stripling, 2009). Similarly, the senior author's own research has detailed experiences of hypersurveillance and supravisibility for Black male academics (Griffin & Reddick, 2011; Reddick & Sáenz, 2012). Black male academics are not exempted from increased scrutiny and microaggressions, whether inside or beyond the ivy walls of campus.

THEORETICAL FRAMEWORK

John Henryism is a physiological term, synonymous with active coping. James, Hartnett, and Kalsbeek (1983) define John Henryism as "an individual's self-perception that he can meet the demands of his environment through hard work and determination" (p. 263). Like the fictional character of American folklore, Black people disposed to John Henryism apply energy and effort to meet the demands of success, but ultimately pay the price through high blood pressure and other illnesses. The idiom familiar to most Black people "you must work twice as hard to go half as far" is rooted deep in Black American culture, and particularly idealized as a means for success among Black men. As Dressler and colleagues wrote in a study on John Henryism and blood pressure among African Americans:

> For men, behaving in terms of John Henryism is virtually the only way of achieving cultural expectations of success under a system of racial stratification, but given the pervasive and pernicious effects of racial discrimination, it is evident that for many black men this tenacious coping style is not enough to overcome the structural barriers in society. For men, the end result is higher blood pressure. (Dressler, Bindon, & Neggers, 1998, p. 623)

I intend to extrapolate this physiological term to the sociocultural environment. I posit that these same traits impact how Black male academics navigate their worlds, with implicit pressures to excel in all the domains which they occupy. These behaviors, in fact, are emblematic of masculine self-reliance (Levant et al., 1992), which centers on autonomy and independent decision making (Addis & Mahalik, 2003; Matthews, Hammond, Nuru-Jeter, Cole-Lewis, & Melvin, 2013). Researchers have examined the effects of John Henryism and racial discrimination, concluding that it creates psychological "wear and tear" (McEwen, 2004; Matthews et al., 2013). This form of coping is a useful way of interpreting and understanding the lived experience of Black male academics leading in their homes and in their communities. The data we derive for this analysis will be a form of autoethnography, scholarly personal narrative [SPN] (Nash, 2004).

METHODOLOGY

We will bring these vignettes to life via scholarly personal narrative (SPN), "a 'counter-narrative' to the faceless, de-contextualized research paradigm that has dominated scholarship in the professional schools for much of the past century" (Nash, 2004, p. vii). In particular, this method is well suited for scholars engaged in inquiry about the experiences of underrepresented populations in the professoriate, as Nash states that these scholars of color "have had to suppress their strong, distinct voices along with their anger, for years in the academy" (p. 2).

While sharing epistemological origins with autoethnographic methods, such as vulnerable anthropology (Behar, 1996), autobiographical ethnography (Glesne, 1998), and scholarly memoir (Willard-Traub, 2001), Nash states that the goal of SPN is to "make narrative sense of personal experience" (2004, p. 18) by "tak[ing] qualitative research one major step further [putting] the *self* of the scholar front and center" (p.18). The narratives forthwith are the senior author's best recollection of experiences with other Black male academics; over the seven years spent in the academy at a research-intensive PWI in the Southern U.S., he considers these interactions and dialogues among the most valued experiences he recounts. We have embraced SPN as a method because it enables us to bring these issues into the academic discourse; with respect to the brothers the senior author has engaged in dialogue with, we have camouflaged their research and other identifiable characteristics and assigned them pseudonyms. We relate this discussion with the full admission that the senior author's interpretation of their words comes from his recall; the errors inherent in this reflection are his alone.

FINDINGS

We have organized the findings surrounding the phenomenon of John Henryism in three categories: *handlin' my bidness at home,* in which Black male academics discuss partner/spousal relationships and fatherhood (both biological/adoptive and fictive); *staying Black in the PWI,* maintaining cultural integrity while striving for advancement and recognition in the "ivory tower" of academe; and *being seen in the community,* negotiating leadership and visibility in spaces in the urban context, but also in a more figurative sense. This section presents vignettes of the senior author's experiences.

Handlin' My Bidness at Home

It was a late summer day in Central Texas—just hot enough to keep folks inside, but not prohibiting a stream of kids and self-anointed grill masters from cycling in and out the house. The house is the home of the Kendricks, the social hub of this group of Black academics. Six or so families are part of this group, which occasionally expands to include others. However, the core group is fairly consistent; these five families are traditional nuclear families, each with one or two children. For the Kendricks (one child) and the Bryants (two children), both partners in these families are involved in the life of the university, with the husbands in tenured or tenure-track position, and the wives working in an administrative capacity in the institution (headed by another Black male senior administrator). For the Okafors (two children) and the Diamonds (two children), both spouses are tenured or tenure-track faculty; in each instance, the couples are in the same academic areas. The Wests (two children) have the husband in a tenured position and the wife working in a nonprofit organization (see Table 1 for a description of the Black male academics in the sample).

Table 1: *"The Brothers"*

Name	Spouse	Number of children	Academic rank	Ethnic background
Mike Kendrick	Stella	1	Associate professor	African American
Will Bryant	Jill	2	Assistant professor	African American/ Caribbean American
Kwame Okafor	Diana	2	Full professor	African American
Lamar Diamond	Sela	2	Associate professor	African American/ Caribbean American
Melvin West	Dominica	2	Associate professor	African American/ Latino

The discussion started with typical kvetching about departmental work: not having time to write enough, being late on book and journal deadlines, and recalcitrant colleagues refusing to pick up the slack. At one point, Kwame Okafor noted that "all of these commitments are eating into my time at home with the family." Will Bryant responded that it was impossible to work at home, because the children demanded constant attention, both positive and negative. Mike Kendrick joked, "We're so busy, we don't even bother trying to keep this place tidy. Y'all have been here enough to know how we live!" While the tone of the discussion was lighthearted, it was evident that each man prioritized his home—marriage, childrearing, and household responsibilities. At the same time, it was also clear that this was a source of strain. Academic jobs, with the constant churn of research projects, mentoring students, and administrative commitments, had a significant, possibly even equivalent, pull on the men's lives. So which side won? In Will's words, "I ain't raising no knuckleheads. I have to be there to lay down the law, because Jill [wife] isn't as consistent as me. These kids will exploit any weaknesses!" Similarly, Lamar Diamond related how his eldest son was involved in a number of sports and activities, and with no immediate family nearby, both he and Sela [wife] were responsible for taking their boy to the events, as well as keeping up with his performance in each activity.

The conversation then moved to a discussion of being significant presences in the men's children's lives. Recognizing that their fathers were of a different generation, each man discussed how their fathers were breadwinners, disciplinarians, and present—but in a different way. Kwame noted that the academic lifestyle made it possible for him to schedule his day to be present for activities and parts of the day that perhaps his father could not do. Melvin West stated that he was able to combine work and family time effectively: "We go to a resort, and I'll be poolside watching the kids, and writing an article. It works great, and everybody's happy." As the talk continued, Lamar introduced another issue: the responsibility of being the family "success story":

"In my extended family, I might be the only man with a degree and no kids out of wedlock. So my siblings and cousins, they're always telling their kids to 'talk to your Uncle Lamar.' I know the importance of this, and it's important, but I'm not always comfortable in that position."

Mike Kendrick agreed: "We have my sister's kids here for a few weeks in the summer, to give her some stability, and let her have access to a middle-class lifestyle for some time." Soon, each man raised examples of "otherfathering" they performed with extended family, church members—as professors, they occupied an elevated status in their families' perspectives. The nod of heads and gentle "I know that's rights" conveyed that these brothers understood that these obligations were part of the package of being successful Black men; it would be unthinkable to "put on airs" or "forget where they came from."

These Black men defined success as keeping a cohesive and functional home life intact, as well as striving for excellence in their professional careers. Nobody suggested that one was more important than the other, though it was clear that the men took advantage of the flexibility inherent in academic life to be present at their children's activities and other family events. These examples of being present extended beyond the nuclear family to relatives and members of the community, such as church members, who called on the men, expecting them to counsel and impart words of wisdom to young people. This service was part and parcel of being successful Black men.

"Staying Black" in the PWI

Will Bryant was one year away from submitting his tenure and promotion materials. Invariably, the conversation moved toward advice from the tenured brothers. Will utilized a family-friendly clock stoppage for the birth of his youngest child, and had the benefit of a fellowship year to bolster his scholarship. Despite this, Will was eager to point out deficiencies he thought others would harp on: the types of journals he elected to publish in and his significant service to the university community (potentially at a cost of doing more research). With this community of Black men, there was complete support for Will's case. As many of the men noted, Will appeared to have a preordained path to tenure. Seeing as Will was a graduate of the institution, Kwame noted: "Man, you'll probably end up being here forever." This evolved into a gentle ribbing of Will for being so concerned about what seemed to be a sure thing.

Each brother gave advice. What was most striking was the fact that the counsel tended to offer ways to meet the standard for tenure that would preserve Will's cultural integrity. Melvin had previously co-authored manuscripts with Will; Mike offered publishing opportunities in a journal on which he served as an editor; and Lamar volunteered to help Will as a proofreader for current submissions. In this way, the community of Black male academics came to resemble the proverbial village helping to raise a child, in this case, to help a Black man achieve tenure.

The advice centered on appropriate venues for publication. Lamar, for instance, had reviewed for a prestigious journal, had work accepted by that journal, and advised Will on the methodologies and frameworks that the journal tended to be amenable to. Mike cautioned Will about publishing too many articles in a journal that was focused on underrepresented populations, but also noted, "Bottom line, you gotta have the numbers, brother." This led to a discussion of how to best present service commitments on Will's vita. Given the research-intensive nature of the institution, Black faculty often find that many of the activities that validate their presence in the academy are actually not as valued in tenure and promotion processes. The tenured men advised Will how to list his service activities in the best possible light. Such an approach allowed Will to "stay Black"—remain rooted in his work with the Black community and maintain legitimacy—concerns that seem prevalent among Black academics in predominantly White institutions (Reddick, Bukoski, Smith, Valdez, & Wasielewski, 2014).

Invariably, the issue of legitimacy has bearing on one's journey to tenure; however, in the conversation, the issue of the importance of having "internal validity" among the Black community at the University came to light. Will recalled a comment from Horace, a senior colleague in the ethnic studies department: "Horace says that ethnic studies can help in tenure cases, but it's only when people are 'known.'"

Mike responded, "What does 'known' mean?"

Will recounted, "Horace went through all of the Black faculty that didn't get tenure in the past few years. Every single one wasn't 'known' by the department. That is, they didn't affiliate with the department, didn't do service or teach in the department, and the department couldn't advocate or write letters of support for tenure." Will's retelling of Horace's words revealed that those faculty who "made themselves known" to the Ethnic Studies Department could additionally benefit from support, not only for their service to the department, but also by having scholars who are perhaps more familiar and place greater value on the intellectual contributions of Black faculty research. While the decision to affiliate with the Ethnic Studies Department was a personal one, the evidence to date suggested that those Black faculty members who did not find a connection to the department faced significant hurdles at tenure and promotion.

Contrary to some thoughts suggesting that Black academic men must bend to the will of the predominantly White institution, these Black faculty members used networks and mentoring tactics to eke out an existence that permitted them to conduct research focused on, and of value to, the Black community. Thus, they did not to surrender aspects of their identity to be successful at the university. In fact, promotion and tenure experiences over the years suggested that it was actually beneficial for Black faculty to teach, serve, or otherwise affiliate with the Ethnic Studies Department, whose leaders could legitimize and comment on the significance of Black men's research agendas, which ultimately led to successful tenure and promotion cases.

Being Seen in the Community

These Black male academics all held roles in the community, such as in fraternal organizations, school boards, civic organizations, and churches. The temptation to "be ghost" and invest oneself in academic pursuits wholly was simply not accepted by the men in this group. As Banks (1984) detailed, "community folk seize on the presence of a rare Black face on the faculty and assume an accompanying sensitivity and moral commitment" (p. 329). These men seemed to understand that being visible in the community was an aspect of being granted the opportunity to hold a position of prestige in the community writ large, and especially the Black community. Mike noted that being a Black male academic "means we are expected to give back…we are standing on the shoulders of giants. Many people made it possible for us to have this privilege." This was a commonly held belief in the group, as several recounted experiences taking leadership in organizations. Kwame added, "When you show up a few times to [an organization], people start assuming that you're going to take a leadership role. You know, 'cause you're a professor. They figure you want to lead folks!"

Will found this attention invigorating and inspiring:

> I mean, I like it, man. I guess I have a lot to say about how things ought to be done. It is kind of nice that people see you in this light, and there's respect with it. Even though my expertise is in one direction, people tend to defer to you, or at least hear you out, because you're the scholar. I guess it can be too much, but I guess I'd rather be in this position than have people telling me what I should be doing.

Both Mike and Kwame held prominent positions in national organizations, and as a result, they often had speaking engagements and meetings out of town

(Mike, in particular, had evaluation responsibilities in different cities and traveled frequently across the state and region). Their leadership seemed to be a manifestation of both their passion for the organizations' missions and their desire to see their values respected in leadership. Mike noted, "Sometimes if I don't make mention of how the organization looks in leadership, people don't say anything. If I'm in the position, things change." Kwame's reputation in his subfield was well-known; he had published scholarship focused on Black populations in the most selective journals in the discipline. His organization had very clear "fingerprints" regarding his leadership.

Lamar held positions in his church, noting the commitment of time required, not just on Sunday, but during the week as well. This spurred someone in the group to bring up that two Black male full professors in their extended social circle were pastors in churches as well. Will said, "Man, I guess those brothers don't have enough on their plates at work," with laughter following. Another Black male senior administrator held a lay position in his church, one man related.

School boards occupied a lot of the men's time. Melvin and Mike served on the same board, and Melvin in particular was actively recruiting Will and Kwame to an open position on the board. Will served on the board of a new school with Sela, Lamar's wife. In addition to their academic roles and responsibilities, the men found ways to apply their knowledge and skills in a concrete manner.

Lamar returned to the issue of serving as a role model and his visibility. "Sometimes it's hard," he remarked. "People want parts of your time, and there's only so much that goes around." The men generally agreed, sharing stories of being held up as examples of "good brothers," while feeling that they were deficient or neglectful of other aspects of their lives. Lamar further brought forth the idea that Black academic men, like John Henry of Americana folklore, were expected to chip away at the rock face of inequity with both arms swinging—to the point of collapse and death. Perhaps the death imagery is grandiose, but the idea that this level of performance came at extensive cost was understood. All of the Black men nodded in agreement, until Melvin said, "That's never happened to me."

Kwame asked, "You've never felt that you had to represent in a manner that wore you down?" Melvin replied, "I can't say that I have." The vibrant, animated discussion grew silent, perhaps through disbelief or shock. "I'm really sorry you have to endure that," Melvin said. His comment moved the conversation to a conclusion, and the moments of connection dissolved into calls after children, the collecting of serving plates, and jingling of keys. In an instant, Mike, Will, Kwame, Lamar, and Melvin returned to their roles as fathers and husbands, as they wrapped up a cathartic conversation that ended on a jarring note.

A major commonality between the Black male professors was their engagement and participation on boards, clubs, and other community activities. Their extensive and prominent engagement suggests that they bore an expectation for leadership and visibility beyond their professional positions. While virtually all the men felt a pressure to perform at a high level, one shared that this burden was not universal.

DISCUSSION & IMPLICATIONS

The research literature is rife with evidence that Black men are subject to excessive pressure in navigating a social reality that limits life opportunity, economic vitality, and their freedom (Pieterse & Carter, 2007; Smith, 2004). However, one might contend that social status and education mitigate these stressors. This narrative reflection suggests that Black male academics aspire to master the demands of their lives as role models, family men, and exemplary scholars through their self-determination and effort (James, Hartnett, & Kalsbeek, 1983). What is most interesting about these vignettes presented in this chapter is that these men did not seek relief from these stressors; in some ways, they seemed to thrive on them, even making light of them on occasion, vividly exhibiting self-reliant orientations (Levant et al., 1992). However, the act of discussing their lives and the efforts involved in maintaining a successful visage appeared to provide something of a safety valve for these Black male professors.

Family (spouses, children, and extended family) were at the forefront of the men's discussion, acknowledging the importance of not only doing this work well for those in their immediate family, but also for those they encountered in other aspects of their lives. In addition, Black male professors in the predominantly White institutional environment expressed how important it was that they meet the demands of academic promotion and advancement, yet not sacrifice their cultural integrity in the process. Kipling's (1910) musing, "If you can talk with crowds and keep your virtue/Or walk with kings—nor lose the common touch," seems analogous to this experience.

As an extension of this concept, Black male professors in this narrative presented their commitment to serving the community. Rather than noting it as an absolute burden, some of the men discussed how they leveraged the expectations upon them as a method of exerting leadership and impacting the direction of the organizations they participated in. While most of the men could empathize with the pressures of leading and participating, at least one man felt that he was able to opt out of such pressures.

If John Henryism is a prevalent method of coping for Black men, and in this case, Black male academics, it would seem that providing forums such as this to allow men to discuss their experiences is a particularly engaging way to vent the pressure that builds. Encouraging Black male academics to enter into fellowship, where the commonalities of their experiences can be shared, may alleviate stresses that are inherently borne by this population. Additional awareness of the tendency for some high-achieving Black men to carry the burden of success in a racially stratified society may help Black male academics to manage their stress in a more productive way. It is telling that a number of the men discussed their membership in faith communities, as there are inspirational passages that proffer appropriate advice: "Come to me, all you that are weary and are carrying heavy burdens, and I will give you rest" (Matthew 11:28 New Revised Standard).

To bring this chapter full circle, it is meaningful to return to the original version of "Brothers Gonna Work It Out":

> And to give an equal share and until you give it him back there'll be no peace
> Brother's gonna work it out brother's gonna work it all out (Hutch, 1973)

REFERENCES

Addis, M. E., & Mahalik, J. R. (2003). Men, masculinity, and the contexts of help-seeking. *American Psychologist, 58*, 5–14.

Allen, W. R., Epps, E. G., Guillory, E. A., Suh, S. A., & Bonous-Hammarth, M. (2000). The Black academic: Faculty status among African Americans in U.S. higher education. *Journal of Negro Education, 69*(1/2), 112–127.

Amber, J. (2013, July 29). The talk: How parents raising Black boys try to keep their sons safe. *TIME*. Retrieved from http://content.time.com/time/magazine/article/0,9171,2147710,00.html

American Council on Education. (2005). *An agenda for excellence: Creating flexibility in tenure-track faculty careers* (Executive summary). Washington, DC: American Council on Education, Office of Women in Higher Education.

Astin, A. W., & Oseguera, L. (2005). *Degree attainment rates at American colleges and universities* (Rev. ed.). Los Angeles, CA: Higher Education Research Institute, UCLA.

Banks, W. M. (1984). Afro-American scholars in the university. *American Behavioral Scientist, 27*(3), 325–338.

Behar, R. (1996). *The vulnerable observer: Anthropology that breaks your heart*. Boston: Beacon Press.

Dressler, W. W., Bindon, J. R., & Neggers, Y. H. (1998). John Henryism, gender, and arterial blood pressure in an African American community. *Psychosomatic Medicine, 60*(5), 620–624.

DuBois, J. (2014, February 9). From Emmett Till to Jordan Davis, a foolish, lethal fear of Black teens. *The Daily Beast*. Retrieved from http://www.thedailybeast.com/articles/2014/02/09/from-emmett-till-to-jordan-davis-a-foolish-lethal-fear-of-black-teens.html

Glesne, C. E. (1998). Ethnography with a biographic eye. In C. A. Kridel (Ed.), *Writing educational biography: Explorations in qualitative research* (pp. 33–44). New York: Garland Publishing.

Griffin, K. A., & Reddick, R. J. (2011). Surveillance and sacrifice: Gender differences in the mentoring patterns of Black professors at predominantly White research universities. *American Educational Research Journal, 48*(5), 1032–1057. doi: 10.3102/0002831211405025.

Harlow, R. (2003). "Race doesn't matter, but...": The effect of race on professors' experiences and emotion management in the undergraduate college classroom. *Social Psychology Quarterly, 66*, 348–363.

Haycock, K., Lynch, M., & Engle, J. (2010). *Opportunity adrift: Our flagship universities are straying from their public mission*. Washington, DC: Education Trust.

Hendrix, K. G. (1998). Student perceptions of the influence of race on professor credibility. *Journal of Black Studies, 28,* 738–763.

Hutch, W. K. (1973). Brothers gonna work it out. On *The Mack* [CD]. Los Angeles, CA: Motown Record Corporation.

Jackson, R., & Crawley, R. (2003). White student confessions about a Black male professor: A cultural contracts theory approach to intimate conversation about race and worldview. *Journal of Men's Studies, 12,* 25–41.

James, S. A., Hartnett, S. A., & Kalsbeek, W. D (1983). John Henryism and blood pressure differences among black men. *Journal of Behavioral Medicine, 6*(3), 259–278.

Kipling, R. (1910). If–. In *Rewards and fairies—Brother square toes*. London, UK: Macmillan.

Levant, R., Hirsch, L., Celentano, E., Cozza, T., Hill, S., MacEachern, M., Marty, N., & Schnedeker, J. (1992). The male role: An investigation of contemporary norms. *Journal of Mental Health Counseling, 14,* 325–337.

Matthews, D. D., Hammond, W. P., Nuru-Jeter, A., Cole-Lewis, Y., & Melvin, T. (2013). Racial discrimination and depressive symptoms among African-American men: The mediating and moderating roles of masculine self-reliance and John Henryism. *Psychology of Men and Masculinity, 14*(1), 35–46.

McEwen, B. S. (2004). Protection and damage from acute and chronic stress: Allostasis and allostatic overload and relevance to the pathophysiology of psychiatric disorders. *Annals of the New York Academy of Sciences, 1032,* 1–7.

Nash, R. J. (2004). *Liberating scholarly narrative: The power of personal narrative*. New York, NY: Teachers College Press.

Pieterse, A. L., & Carter, R. T. (2007). An examination of the relationship between general life stress, racism-related stress, and psychological health among Black men. *Journal of Counseling Psychology, 54*(1), 101–109.

Reddick, R. J., Bukoski, B. E., Smith, S. L., Valdez, P. L., & Wasielewski, M. V. (2014). A hole in the soul of Austin: Black faculty community engagement experiences in a creative class city. *Journal of Negro Education, 83*(1), 61-76.

Reddick, R. J., & Sáenz, V. B. (2012). Coming home: *Hermanos académicos* reflect on paths and present realities at their home institution. *Harvard Educational Review, 82*(3), 353–380.

Reddick, R. J., & Vincent, G. J. (2014, August 25). Commentary: Black youth should be nurtured, not targeted. *Austin American-Statesman*. Retrieved from http://www.mystatesman.com/news/news/opinion/commentary-black-youth-should-be-nurtured-not-targ/ng8Zs/

Robertson, C., & Schwartz, J. (2012, March 22). Trayvon Martin death spotlights neighborhood watch groups. *New York Times*. Retrieved from http://www.nytimes.com/2012/03/23/us/trayvon-martin-death-spotlights-neighborhood-watch-groups.html?_r=2&

Shocklee, H., Sadler, E., & Ridenhour, C. (1990). Brothers gonna work it out On *Fear of a Black planet* [CD]. New York, NY: Def Jam Recordings and Columbia Records.

Smith, W. A. (2004). Black faculty coping with racial battle fatigue: The campus racial climate in a post-civil rights era. In D. Cleveland (Ed.), *A long way to go: Conversations about race by African American faculty and graduate students* (pp. 191–210). New York, NY: Peter Lang Publishing.

Solórzano, D., Ceja, M., & Yosso, T. (2000). Critical race theory, racial microaggressions, and campus racial climate: The experiences of African American college students, *Journal of Negro Education, 69*(1/2), 60–73.

Stripling, J. (2009). News: If it can happen to him... Retrieved from http://www.insidehighered.com/news/2009/07/22/gates

Thompson, G. L., & Louque, A. (2005). *Exposing the "culture of arrogance" in the academy: A blueprint for increasing Black faculty satisfaction.* Sterling, VA: Stylus.

Tuitt, F. A., Hanna, M., Martinez, L. M., del Carmen Salazar, M. C., & Griffin, R. A. (2009). Teaching in the line of fire: Faculty of color in the academy. *Thought & Action, 24,* 65–74.

U.S. Census and U.S. Bureau of Labor Statistics. (2013). Current population survey: Educational attainment in the United States. Retrieved from http://www.census.gov/hhes/socdemo/education/data/cps/2013/Table%201-04.xlsx

Whitaker, F., Bongiovi, N. Y. (Producers), & Coogler, R. (Director) (2014). *Fruitvale Station* [Motion picture]. United States: Anchor Bay Entertainment.

Willard-Traub, M. (2001). *Personal effects: The social character of scholarly writing.* Logan, UT: Utah State University Press.

CHAPTER FIVE

The State of Health Among Black Men in the United States: Implications of Demographic Heterogeneity

JUANITA J. CHINN AND ANDREA K. HENDERSON

The health of Black men is a growing but understudied public health concern. It is well known that Black men in the United States suffer some of the worst health outcomes, including higher rates of heart disease, diabetes, and premature mortality (Williams, 2003). A host of structural issues have contributed to the disparate health trajectories of Black men, including educational attainment and incarceration (Williams, 2003). However, much of the work on the intersectionality of race, gender, and health has largely ignored the issue of intra-ethnic heterogeneity within the Black racial category. Immigration from Africa and the Caribbean has changed the face of Black America. At least 20% of the growth in the U.S. Black population between 2001 and 2006 was due to immigration (Kent, 2007). In some areas of the country, including New York, Miami, and Boston, Black immigrants comprise more than one-fourth of the Black population (Kent, 2007). A myriad of structural issues have contributed to the influx of Black immigration, including political and economic forces. The use of the monolithic category "African American" obscures the growing diversity among Blacks in the United States and as a consequence, little is known about health—both physical and mental health—differences among native-born and foreign-born Blacks.

This chapter has several purposes. First, we begin by broadly reviewing the current literature on the demographic trends related the health status of Black men[1] in the United States. In this chapter, we define health as encompassing both physical and mental well-being, similar to the definition provided by the World Health Organization (WHO, 1946). Second, as a contribution to the literature, we will examine nativity differences as they correlate to multiple physical and mental health outcomes across key demographic characteristics (i.e., age, marital status, education level, and income) among nationally representative samples of Black men residing in the United States. We conclude by reviewing the literature on the social and cultural determinants of Black men's health in the United States.

PHYSICAL HEALTH

HIV/AIDS and Black Men

Today, more than 1.1 million people are living with HIV/AIDS in the United States. Black Americans account for more than half of those cases. Since the start of the epidemic, Black Americans have been disproportionately affected by the disease and these disparities have widened over time. In addition, in 2010, Black Americans accounted for 44% of new cases of HIV, and Black men were the population most significantly impacted (Centers for Disease Control [CDC], 2012). The rate of new HIV infection among Black men is 7 times that of White men, twice that of Latino men, and nearly 3 times as high as Black women (CDC, 2012). Among Black men, men who have sex with men (MSM) are at greatest risk of infection. In 2006, Black MSM represented 63% of new infections among all Black men, and 35% among all MSM. Moreover, new HIV infections occurred primarily among young Black MSM (ages 13–29) more than any other age and racial group of MSM (CDC, 2012).

Several explanations have been posited for the elevated rates of HIV among Black men. First, smaller sexual networks make the transmission rate higher among Black MSM (Millett, Peterson, Wolitski, & Stall, 2006; Ruiz, Facer, & Sun, 1998; Service & Blower, 1995). That is, Black MSMs are more likely to have sex with other Black male partners, which increases their risk of infection. Second, socioeconomic disadvantage is another key component in the high prevalence of HIV in the Black community. Higher rates of poverty, racial discrimination, and access to quality care are key determinants in the health disparities of Black men (Millett et al., 2006). Third, differences in testing practices, including prolonged periods without testing, has been identified as an important component in this growing health disparity (CDC, 2002; Millett et al., 2006). In addition to HIV, physical health encompasses a variety of outcomes, including infant and adult morbidity and mortality. Several of these outcomes will be explored below.

Infant Health and Mortality

Infant mortality refers to deaths that occur to persons who are less than one year old. The most important measure of infant mortality among populations is the number of infant deaths per 1,000 live births in a population during a given year. The infant mortality rate is often considered to be a key measure of the overall health and well-being of a population (Frisbie, 2005).

Black Americans have infant mortality rates (IMR) that are more than double the IMRs of White and Hispanics in the United States. In the U.S., the infant mortality rate is 6.6 deaths per 1,000 live births (Mathews & MacDorman, 2012). For non-Hispanic Whites, this rate is even lower, at 5.5/1000. However, for non-Hispanic Blacks, this rate is 12.7 infant deaths per 1,000 births (Mathews & MacDorman, 2012). Given the importance of the IMR as an indicator of the overall health of a population, it is evident that a clear racial disparity in the health of Americans exists, with Blacks in the United States at a stark disadvantage. Moreover, there is a history of evidence pointing to a gender disparity in infant mortality with male babies experiencing higher rates of death (Drevenstedt, Crimmins, Vasunilashorn, & Finch, 2008). However, Black male infants experience the worst rates of infant mortality relative to any other race/gender combination in the United States (Arias, 2012).

This same racial disparity is apparent when examining other infant health outcomes, including infant birth weight and rate of preterm births. Infant birth weight is used as an indicator of clinical disease risk and infant mortality (World Health Organization, 1946). Low birth weight is defined as the percentage of live-born infants with birth weight less than 2,500g (approximately 5 lbs 8 oz.) in a given time period. Blacks in the United States experience double the rates of low birth weight compared to their White and Hispanic counterparts, but they also experience a greater rate of survival at a given low weight birth (Wilcox & Russell, 1990). Preterm births are classified as births of an infant at less than 37 weeks gestational age. Infants born prematurely are at greater risks of infant mortality and other health complications both in the short term and across the life course (Braveman & Barclay, 2009). Blacks experience preterm births at 1.5 times the rate of Whites. Blacks have a preterm birth prevalence rate of 17.1%, while Whites have a 10.8% prevalence rate (Martin et al., 2012).

Child and Young Adult Health and Mortality

The age range in which one's health and mortality are classified as child mortality varies (Frisbie, Hummer, & McKinnon, 2009). In this chapter, child mortality is defined as a death occurring between the ages of 1 and 14. Child deaths will be separated into two categories, ages 1–4 and ages 5–14. Ages 5–14 have the lowest death rates and best health experiences throughout the life course across all racial groups. In addition, this section will include information on young adult (ages 15–24) health and mortality.

Mortality (or death) rates are expressed as the number of deaths occurring per 100,000 people in a given age group. The data presented in Table 5.1 are the child and young adult mortality rates for U.S. Black males and comparison populations as of 2010 (Murphy, Xu, & Kochanek, 2013). These data were published by the National Center for Health Statistics.

Table 5.1. Child and Young Adult Mortality Rates per 100,000 for U.S. Black Men and Comparison Populations, 2010.

Panel A: Men

Age Group	NH Black[a]	NH White	Hispanic	Total U.S.
1–4	45.4	27.5	25.0	29.6
5–14	20.7	14.3	11.4	14.6
15–24	150.8	93.4	79.4	97.6

Panel B: Women

Age Group	NH Black	NH White	Hispanic	Total U.S.
1–4	34.8	21.8	20.2	23.3
5–14	15.5	10.9	8.9	11.1
15–24	45.6	38.4	26.3	36.4

Note. Adapted from the report by Murphy et al. (2013).
[a] Non-Hispanic

The most common cause of death among children, across races, is accidental death. There is a racial disparity in the death rates among children; Black male children are at the greatest disadvantage. However, this racial disparity is not nearly as large as it is for young adults. For young adults, the leading causes of death are accidents, homicide, and suicide (Murphy et al., 2013). For Black men ages 15–24, the leading cause of death is homicide and for their White counterparts, it is accidents (Murphy et al., 2013). Overall, there is a larger gender gap in mortality for this age group as well (see Table 5.1). Generally, men have death rates that are more than double the rate of women. For Blacks, this gender disparity is much greater, with Black men experiencing more than 3 times the death rates of Black women.

Adult Mortality and Life Expectancy

Black men experience a lower life expectancy at birth than any other racial/ethnic/sex group in the United States (data available for Blacks, Hispanics, and Whites only) (Arias, 2012). Black men live, on average, at least 6 fewer years than other racial/ethnic/sex groups. Life expectancy for Black men at birth is 70.6 years. This is almost 7 years fewer than Black women, who have a life expectancy of 77.2 years. Hayward and Heron (1999) found that, in 1990, a 20-year-old Black man could expect to live an additional 47 years, 9 of which would be spent disabled. In contrast, a 20-year-old White man in 1990 would live on average an additional 54.6 years, 8 of which would be spent disabled. Essentially, a White man will live longer, and spend less time (proportionally and in absolute years) disabled.

Table 5.2. Life Expectancy at Birth (in Years) by Race and Sex as of 2008.

Sex	Black	White	Hispanic
Male	70.56	76.05	78.39
Female	77.17	80.90	83.35

Note. Adapted from Table A in Arias (2012, p. 3).

Table 5.3 uses the most recent version of official U.S. mortality data (Murphy et al., 2013) to display 2010 age-specific adult mortality rates per 100,000 persons for non-Hispanic Black men and comparison populations. Numerator data for official mortality rates are taken from death certificates, while denominator data are taken from population estimates provided by the U.S. Census Bureau.

Table 5.3. Age-Specific Adult Mortality Rates per 100,000 for U.S. Black Men and Comparison Populations, 2010.
Panel A: Men

Age Group	NH Black	NH White	Hispanic	Total U.S.
25–34	230.8	143.6	100.9	141.5
35–44	321.1	219.1	146.2	212.5
45–54	739.1	508.1	351.9	505.9
55–64	1705.1	1046.2	815.1	1075.5
65–74	3274.7	2256.9	1775.0	2275.1
75–84	6849.1	5770.3	4461.9	5693.7
85+	14974.2	15816.6	11779.8	15414.3
Age-Adjusted Rate a	1131.7	892.5	677.7	887.1

Panel B: Women

Age Group	NH Black	NH White	Hispanic	Total U.S.
25–34	99.1	66.8	38.9	64.0
35–44	209.1	133.1	75.2	128.9
45–54	497.4	307.7	193.9	311.4
55–64	996.9	631.5	450.1	643.5
65–74	2068.1	1535.9	1085.5	1527.5
75–84	4675.5	4232.6	3067.4	4137.7
85+	12767.7	13543.5	10237.3	13219.2
Age-Adjusted Rate [a]	770.8	643.3	463.4	634.9

Note. Adapted from Table 5 in Murphy et al. (2013, p. 27–28).

[a] The age-adjusted death rate standardizes for age structure differences across populations. The age-adjusted mortality rates reported here pertain to the complete life course and not just adult age groups. However, because U.S. mortality is so heavily concentrated in the adult ages, these age-adjusted rates largely reflect the mortality levels of U.S. adults.

It is clear from Table 5.3 that for most age groups, adult mortality rates are higher for non-Hispanic Black men than other racial/sex groups for all age categories, except for individuals age 85 or more years. This is known as the mortality crossover. That is, higher age-specific adult mortality is experienced by Black men and women until around age 85. At which time, non-Hispanic Blacks experience more favorable mortality patterns than their non-Hispanic White counterparts (Nam, Weatherby, & Ockay, 1978). Two primary explanations have been given for this phenomenon. The first explanation notes that the compositions of Black and White populations vary across time and age groups, such that the frailest members of the Black population have experienced mortality during the younger ages. Therefore, the members of the older Black population are the most resilient and robust. Thus, when they reach the oldest age bracket, the Black population will be composed of relatively more robust members that experience lower mortality risk (Lynch, Brown, & Harmsen, 2003; Nam, 1995). The second explanation notes that the mortality crossover pattern is an artifact of low-quality data for people, particularly Black people, age 85 or older (Coale & Kisker, 1986; Preston & Elo, 2006). This explanation suggests that the data, specifically birth records, are not accurate and inflate the actual age of Blacks in the dataset. Studies that test the data quality explanation have found convergence of mortality patterns at much older ages, or no convergence at all. Other studies have shown the mortality crossover pattern to be a result of cohort differences (Masters, 2012).

Gender, Health, and Mortality

The gender paradox in health states that although men have higher rates of mortality, and experience lower life expectancies, women experience greater disability, illness, and poor health (Waldron, 1976; Rieker & Bird, 2005). One explanation is that men and women interpret their current health differently, and therefore men report their health status differently than women, even with the same health status. Additional explanations include: (1) men are less engaged with preventive and health-promoting behaviors than women (Walker, Volkan, Sechrist, & Pender, 1988; Courtenay, 2000); (2) men are employed in more hazardous occupations than women; and (3) some argue that men demonstrate their masculinity by taking risks with their health and/or dismissing their health needs to "legitimize themselves as the 'stronger' sex" (Courtenay, 2000, p. 1397).

Nativity and Morbidity

The immigrant health advantage posits that foreign-born persons experience better health and health outcomes than native-born persons of the same racial/ethnic group (Hummer, Powers, Pullum, Gossman, & Frisbie, 2007; Kaestner, Pearson, Keene, & Geronimus, 2009). Three explanations for this relationship between health and nativity are (1) healthy immigrant selection (Hummer et al., 2007), (2) return migration of the unhealthy migrants (Palloni & Arias, 2004), and (3) inaccurate data records. There is evidence that the immigrant health advantage is not uniform across racial/ethnic groups (Singh & Miller, 2004), or even within group (Read, Emerson, & Tarlov, 2005). In fact, Read et al. (2005) demonstrate that there are distinct health patterns among Black immigrants that are often overlooked. Though we will not parse out nativity by country or region of birth of immigrants, it is important to note the heterogeneity of Black immigrants in the United States. They are of Hispanic and non-Hispanic ethnicity and from countries all over the world, particularly from Africa, the Caribbean, and South America.

In this portion of the chapter, we analyze the most recent data to compare the current state of physical health among Black men in the United States by nativity status, specifically comparing the health conditions of U.S.-born and non-U.S.-born (or foreign-born) males. We use the National Health Interview Survey 2007-2011 Sample Adult Files (NHIS) to determine the probability of seven health conditions by age group (National Center for Health Statistics [NCHS], 2013). The NHIS is an annual cross-sectional household survey of a sample of the non-institutionalized U.S. population. Surveys are administered in person and are completed by the respondent unless otherwise indicated. The NHIS contains an over-sampling of Blacks. The NHIS sample adult supplement contains additional health questions or details not captured in the core NHIS. The NHIS sample adult supplement files surveys one respondent from each household over the age of 17. The current data are restricted to Black men ages 18 or older. The analytic data set contains five years of cross-sectional data, yielding 8,537 adults, with approximately 14% foreign-born Black men.

Table 5.4. Weighted Demographic Characteristics of Black Men Ages 18 and Older by Nativity Status.

Variable	US Born	Foreign Born	Total
Age (Mean Years)	47.0	43.7	46.5
Marital Status			
Married	38.8	56.7	41.3
Unmarried	61.2	43.3	58.7
Education			
More than High Sch	46.2	55.1	47.5
High Sch Graduate	33.6	27.3	32.7
Less Than High Sch	19.0	16.7	18.7
Family Income: Poverty Threshold			
2.00 or More	54.6	55.7	54.7
1.00 – 1.99	18.0	18.1	18.0
0.99 or Less	17.1	16.4	17.0
Missing Poverty Info	10.3	9.7	10.2
Weighted N	8291	1346	9637
UnWeighted N	7380	1157	8537
UnWeighted N (%)	86.4	13.6	100.0

Note. All numbers are percentages unless otherwise stated. Data from the National Health Interview Survey Sample Adult Files, 2007–2011.

We examine multiple demographic measures including age, marital status, education level, and family income to poverty ratio. These weighted descriptive statistics are presented in Table 5.4. On average, Black male immigrants are younger, have higher rates of being married, and higher levels of education than their U.S.-born counterparts. However, these characteristics do not translate into lower rates of poverty. U.S.-born and non-U.S.-born Black men experience similar poverty rates. Approximately 35% of Black men, both U.S. born and non-U.S. born, live in poverty (poverty threshold ratio of 0.99 or less) or near the poverty threshold level (1.00–1.99).

Using these data, we examined seven measures of health: (a) heart disease, (b) all cancers, (c) diabetes, (d) hypertension, (e) body mass index (BMI) greater than or equal to 30.0, (f) fair or poor self-rated health, (g) functional limitations, as well as (h) current smoking status. Heart disease, cancer, and stroke are three leading causes of death in the United States (Murphy et al., 2013) and diabetes disproportionately affects the Black community. The prevalence rates of these diseases are presented in Table 5.5.

BMI is dichotomized as a score of 30 or higher and less than 30, which is the Centers for Disease Control cut point for obesity (CDC, 2010). Functional limitations are defined as restrictions in the performance of fundamental physical and mental activities used in daily life by ones age-sex group (Verbrugge & Jette, 1994; Nagi, 1976). Functional limitations and BMI can serve as a very important indicator of morbidity and health status. The functional limitations variable is a summary variable and refers to an affirmative answer to any one of the 12 functional limitation questions asked of respondents. This includes if the respondent is able to complete the following tasks without assistance: walk a quarter of a mile; walk up 10 steps; stand for 2 hours; sit for two hours; stoop, bend, and/or kneel; reach over head; grasp small objects; lift and carry 10 pounds; push/pull large objects; attend events (e.g., movies, sporting events); go to social activities; and also whether the respondent has difficulty relaxing. Functional limitations are a measure of the physical capabilities of the body. It can be assessed without access to a health care provider and identifies the actual "wear and tear" or deterioration of the body's ability to perform common, everyday tasks. Self-rated health is a dichotomized self-assessment of the respondent's health: poor or fair. It has shown to be a predictor of mortality (Mossey & Shapiro, 1982).

Table 5.5. Prevalence of Health Measures for Black Men Ages 18 and Older by Nativity Status.

Variable	US Born	Foreign Born	Total
Heart Disease	10.0	4.4	9.2
Any Cancer	4.1	1.5	3.7
Diabetes	12.4	9.4	12.0
Hypertension	33.6	24.3	32.3
BMI ≥ 30	33.5	17.6	31.3
Poor/Fair Self Rated Health	17.1	8.2	15.9
Functional Limitation	28.1	14.3	26.2
Current Smoker	26.1	12.0	24.1

Note. All numbers are percentages unless otherwise stated. Data from the National Health Interview Survey Sample Adult Files, 2007–2011.

As expected, the prevalence of each health measure is greater among U.S.-born men than foreign-born men. Part of the disparity may be attributed to the differences in the average ages of the two populations. Nevertheless, the health disparities by nativity are quite drastic for most of the measures analyzed. U.S.-born Black men report having heart disease, any cancer, obesity, functional limitations, and being a current smoker at double (or greater) the rate of foreign-born Black men. However, the nativity disparity is much less for diabetes and hypertension.

It is important to note, as previously mentioned, U.S.-born men are, on average, older than foreign-born men in the sample. This may contribute to the nativity disparity observed in the descriptive data. The data are adjusted for age, education, marital status, and income in the logistic regression results presented in Figure 5.1 and Figure 5.2. These models also control for smoking status. In addition, there is a significant difference between the smoking status of U.S.-born Black men and foreign-born Black men, which may also contribute to the disparities in health observed.

Figure 5.1 displays the predicted probabilities of heart disease, all cancers, diabetes, and hypertension for Black men, ages 18 and older, in the United States by age and nativity status. The predicted probabilities were calculated using logistic regressions and control for educational attainment, poverty level, and marital status. At the youngest ages, the gap, or disparity in health, is minimal; however, they begin to increase during middle age, and begin to close at the oldest ages. This pattern is observed for heart disease, diabetes, and hypertension. However, for all cancers, the health disparity by nativity status does not converge (or begin to converge) at the oldest ages.

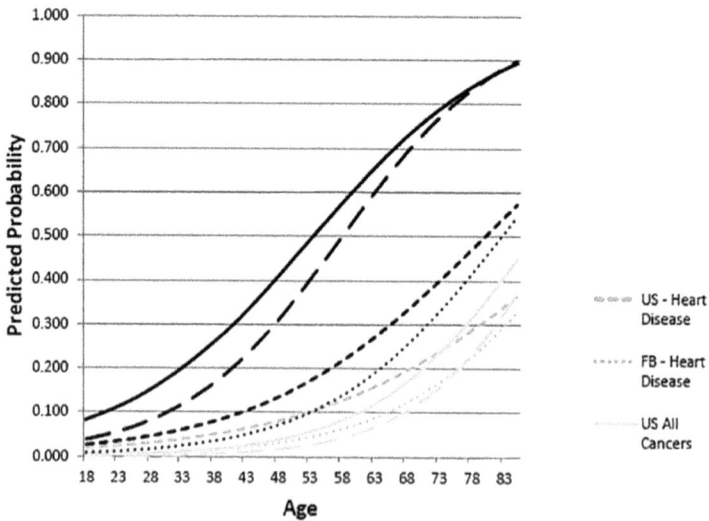

Figure 5.1. Predicted Probabilities of Specific Illness for Black Males by Age and Nativity.
Note: Data from the National Health Interview Survey Sample Adult Files, 2007–2011

Figure 2 displays the predicted probabilities of body mass index greater than or equal to 30 (obesity), fair or poor self-rated health, and functional limitations for Black men in the United States, ages 18 and older, by age and nativity status. The predicted probabilities were calculated using logistic regression and again control for educational attainment, poverty level, marital status, and smoking status. Looking at obesity, the probability of being obese is fairly constant across adulthood of Black men at just above 40%, regardless of nativity status. As expected, the probability of both functional limitations and fair or poor self-rated health increase with age. However, the disparity by nativity status in these two health measures also increases with age. That is, native-born Black men experience higher probability of both negative health outcomes at each age.

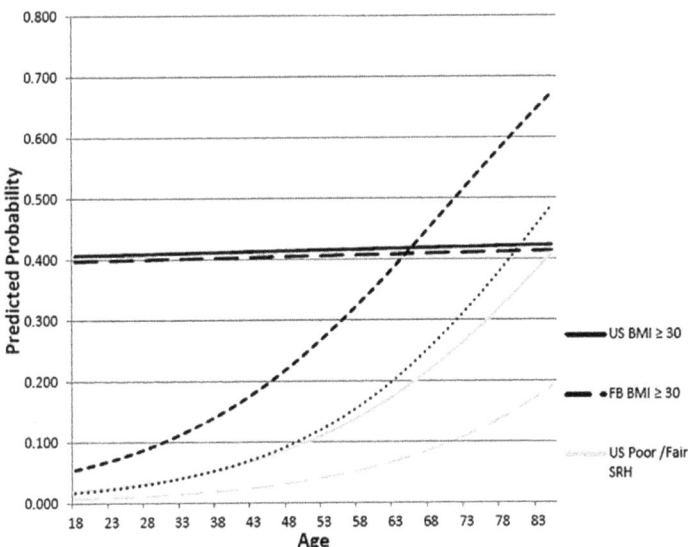

Figure 5.2. Predicted Probabilities of Specific Illness for Black Males by Age and Nativity.
Note: Data from the National Health Interview Survey Sample Adult Files, 2007–2011

MENTAL HEALTH

Mental health is a multifaceted concept that encompasses a broad collection of cognitive, emotional and behavioral phenomena, including mental illness (e.g., depression and anxiety), psychosocial well-being (e.g., life satisfaction and happiness) and self-concept (e.g., self-acceptance and efficacy). A wealth of research suggests that mental health is paramount to educational and occupational attainment, family relationships, and personal and social well-being (Fletcher, 2010; Gross & John, 2003; Hill & Madhere, 1996; Lyons-Ruth, Connell, Grunebaum,

& Botein, 1990). However, a report by the Surgeon General highlighted the vast racial/ethnic disparities in mental health (U.S. DHHS, 2001). In addition, there is strong evidence for Black men being disproportionately affected by poor mental health (Watkins, Walker, & Griffith, 2009; Williams, 2003).

What do we know about racial/ethnic differences in mental health? First, research suggests that Blacks are no more likely to suffer from serious mental illness than Whites, especially once differences in socioeconomic status are controlled (Regier et al., 1993; Robins & Regier, 1991; Zhang & Snowden, 1999). In fact, according to the National Comorbidity Survey—a nationally representative survey of African Americans, Whites, and Hispanics—African Americans have a lower lifetime prevalence of common mental disorders, including mood and anxiety, as well as substance abuse disorders (Kessler et al., 1994; Kessler et al., 1996). Differences were found, however, in the persistence of these disorders. Although Black adults were at no greater risk of developing mental illness, once developed, there was an increased risk that mental illness would persist over the life course (Kessler et al., 1996). The persistence of mental illness speaks largely to a lack of resources in receiving appropriate care for the treatment of mental illness in the Black community (Kessler et al., 1996). The evidence regarding racial/ethnic differences in psychological distress or depressive symptoms is less clear. Several studies suggest that Black Americans fare better on these outcomes, while other studies suggest they do worse (Bratter & Eschbach, 2005; Esmlie et al., 1990; Myers et al., 2002).

When examining gender variation and mental illness among Blacks, we find a similarly complex story. Black women are more likely to report higher rates of depression, anxiety, and phobia compared to Black men (U.S. DHHS, 2006). However, estimates of mental illness among Black men may be under reported in national studies due to the large percentage of Black men in high-need populations, including incarceration, psychiatric hospitalization, and residential isolation. Inclusion of these high-need populations may result in elevated rates of mental illness among Black men (Kessler et al., 2004; Teplin, 1990; U.S. DHHS, 2001; Watkins et al., 2009; Williams, 2003; Williams & Jackson, 2000). Nevertheless, estimates suggest that 2.6% of Black men, ages 18 and over, suffer from serious psychological distress, while an estimated 7% of Black men report a lifetime prevalence of major depressive disorder (U.S. DHHS, 2006; Williams et al., 2007). In addition, there has been a dramatic increase in the suicide rate among Black men, particularly young Black men between the ages of 15 to 24 (U.S. DHHS, 2006). One nationally representative study suggests that among Black men ages 18 years and older an estimated 10.2% have a lifetime prevalence of suicide ideation, and an estimated 2.7% suicide attempt (Joe et al., 2006). The risk of suicide persists into older adulthood resulting in nearly 2,000 deaths annually (McIntosh & Drapeau, 2012).

We also know that there is a shortage of empirical investigation on racial/ ethnic differences in subjective, psychosocial well-being. Among the few studies examining these mental health outcomes, findings suggest Blacks report lower levels of life satisfaction and happiness compared with Whites (Hughes & Thomas, 1998). Additionally, Blacks are more likely to report greater life stress and more stressful life events (Brown et al., 1999; Jackson-Triche et al., 1997). Lower levels of psychosocial well-being among Blacks are related to social and economic disadvantage, which may be especially true for Black men (Han et al., 2006). For example, one study of young African American men in inner-city Baltimore found that a majority of respondents dealt *repeatedly* with the deaths of family members or close friends, housing instability, unemployment, and underemployment. These findings suggest that young African American men face cumulative stressful life events, which negatively impact their mental health (Han et al., 2006).

Lastly, when we turn our attention to subgroup variation in self-concept measures like self-esteem and self-efficacy, research suggests that compared to Whites, Blacks report higher levels of self-acceptance, but lower levels of self-mastery (Adams, 2003; Bruce & Thornton, 2004; Hughes & Thomas, 1998; Shaw & Krause, 2001; Twenge & Crocker, 2002). Specifically, self-esteem refers to one's general feelings of self-worth or self-value, while personal mastery refers to one's beliefs about one's ability to influence and produce events that affect one's environment or life chances (Bandura, 1997). These two dimensions of well-being are thought to stem from social processes, including reflected appraisals (e.g., our perceptions of what others think of us) and mastery experiences (e.g., gaining confidence through experience) (Bandura, 1997; Mead, 1934; Rosenberg, 1986). Blacks are believed to have elevated levels of self-acceptance based on different standards used to judge self-worth (e.g., Black identity formation and social networks), while their lower rates of self-efficacy are attributed to structural disadvantages, including educational and occupational barriers (Buchanan & Gossett, 2002; Gray-Little & Hafdahl, 2000). Moreover, study findings suggest rates of self-efficacy and self-esteem are lower among Black men compared to Black women (Buchanan & Selmon, 2008; Dukes & Martinez, 1994; Rotheram-Borus, Dopkins, Sabate, & Lightfoot, 1996). One study found that the self-esteem of Black boys is less stable than that of their Black female counterparts (Wade, Thompson, Tashakkori, & Valente, 1989). However, more work in the area of subgroup and gender variation and self-concept needs to be done.

Nativity and Mental Health

Structural factors like socioeconomic status, discrimination, and gender socialization are salient in explaining racial and gender differences in mental health, while other factors have largely been ignored, including gender and nativity (Watkins,

Walker, & Griffith, 2009; Williams & Earl, 2007). Findings from the few studies examining the effect of nativity on mental health suggests that the relationship is varied and complex. Results of several studies suggest that foreign-born adults report either no difference or better levels of mental health, including lower rates of mental illness and psychological distress, than U.S.-born adults. For instance, no significant differences were found among native-born and foreign-born Blacks on major depressive disorder, however both groups were more likely to rate their psychological distress more severely and more disabling relative to Whites (Williams et al., 2007). However, gender differences were not explored. In other studies, however, the mental health of foreign-born Blacks is substantially worse than their native-born counterparts, and gender was also found to be a key predictor (Cohen, Berment, & Magai, 1997; Doyle, Joe, & Caldwell, 2012; Gibbs, et al., 2013). For example, Williams et al. (2007), using a nationally representative survey of African American and Afro-Caribbean individuals, found that Caribbean-born Black men had higher risk of 12-month psychiatric disorders than U.S.-born Black men. Future research examining the mental health of Black Americans may seek to explore sociocultural explanations, including nativity, to explain the disparate mental health outcomes.

A New Analysis on Mental Health

In this section, we provide a new analysis on the mental health of Black men in the United States. Data come from The National Survey of American Life: Coping with Stress in the 21st Century (NSAL). The NSAL was collected from 2001 to 2003, by the Program for Research on Black Americans at the University of Michigan's Institute for Social Research. The NSAL was designed to explore racial/ethnic differences in mental disorders, psychological distress, and formal and informal services used among three target populations: African American, Afro-Caribbean, and non-Hispanic White (Jackson et al., 2004a, 2004b). The survey was administered to a sample of non-institutionalized English-speaking adults aged 18 or older. The African American sample is the core sample of the NSAL. However, the NSAL includes the first major probability sample of Caribbean Blacks ever conducted. For the purposes of the survey, Caribbean Blacks were defined as persons who trace their ethnic heritage to a Caribbean country, but who now reside in the United States, are racially classified as Black and who are English-speaking, but may also speak another language (Jackson et al., 2004a, 2004b).

For our purposes, the data was restricted to Black men, including the African American and Afro-Caribbean subsamples, who were 18 years or older at the time of the survey. There are five mental health outcomes selected for analysis. First, *subjective mental health* was assessed using a single item asking respondents to rate their mental health. Response categories ranged from 1 = excellent to 5 = poor, and the item was reverse coded so that higher scores reflect better subjective mental health. Second, *depression* is a scale of four questions regarding the respondent's mood over the past month, including "feeling so depressed nothing could cheer the [respondent] up" and "feeling blue." Response categories ranged from 1 = all of the time to 5 = none of the time and were reverse coded where necessary so that higher scores reflect more depressive symptoms (Cronbach's alpha = .66). The third and fourth measures were *self-esteem* and *self-mastery*. Respondents were asked to select their level of agreement with a series of statements, including "I'm a person of worth," "I've got a lot of good qualities," "I feel pushed around in life," and "I can do just about anything I set my mind to." Response categories ranged from 1 = strongly agree to 4 = strongly disagree, and items were reverse coded where necessary so that higher scores reflect higher levels of self-esteem and self-mastery. The Cronbach's alphas for self-esteem and self-mastery are .80 and .71, respectively. Lastly, *life satisfaction* was measured using a single item and higher scores reflect greater life satisfaction.

Again, we control for multiple demographic measures including age, marital status, education, and family income. These descriptive statistics are presented in Table 5.6. On average, foreign-born Black men have higher rates of marriage/cohabitation, education, and income. There are no significant differences between the two groups in regards to age.

Table 5.6. Demographic Characteristics of Black Males Ages 18 and Older by Nativity Status.

Variable	US Born	Foreign Born	Total
Age (Mean Years)	41.8	40.6	41.8
Marital Status			
Married/Cohabiting	48.8	65.8	50.3
Unmarried	31.1	22.1	30.4
Education			
More Than High School	36.7	55.3	38.3
High School Graduate	39.4	30.7	38.6
Less Than High School	23.9	14.0	23.1
Income (Mean dollars)	42,013.98	47,183.60	42406.17
N	1398	494	1914

Data from the National Survey of American Life (NSAL)
Data are weighted.

Table 5.7 presents mean scores to illustrate nativity differences in the mental health of Black men. Mean estimates were generated using general linear models (GLM) procedure in SAS. The mean differences adjust for the demographic controls. The results reveal that on average the mental health of native-born

Black men is significantly different from foreign-born Black men on several key measures. Significant differences were evident across three of the five measures of mental health. Specifically, the results suggest that U.S.-born Black men report lower levels of self-mastery on average than foreign-born Black men, but higher levels of self-esteem and life satisfaction. No significant differences were found between subjective mental health and depressive symptomology. These results highlight the important, but often overlooked, role of nativity status in understanding the mental health of the Black community

Table 5.7. Mean Levels of Mental Health by Nativity Status

	Range	US Born	Foreign Born
Subjective Mental Health	1-5	3.93	4.05
Depression	1-5	1.68	1.65
Self-Esteem	1-4	3.57	3.50*
Self-Mastery	1-4	3.15	3.37***
Life Satisfaction	1-4	3.27	3.08***

Data from the National Survey of American Life (NSAL)
Nativity differences significant at: +p<.10; * p<.05;** p<.01;*** p<.001
Means are adjusted for the effects of age, education, income and marital status
Data are weighted.

DETERMINANTS OF HEALTH

Research suggests there are several key social and cultural determinants when considering the health disadvantage of Black men. Four key determinants are discussed herein. First, race represents the interconnectivity of "biological factors, geographic origins, culture, economic, political and legal factors as well as racism" (Williams, 1996). That is, race has been and continues to be a determining factor in the collective condition of racial minorities in the United States (Hummer & Chinn, 2011). For instance, socioeconomic status (SES) is one of the strongest determinants of health, whether measured by income, education, or occupation (Williams, 1996; Hayward Crimmins, Miles, & Yang, 2000; Hummer & Chinn, 2011). Low-SES men are at a greater risk of developing health problems (Hayward & Heron, 1999; Hummer and Chinn, 2011). When examining racial differences in mortality outcomes, Hummer and Chinn (2011) found that socioeconomic resources accounted for a large portion of the racial differences in mortality. However, they argue that these socioeconomic differences reflect the historical and continuing effects of race and racial stratification in the United States. In essence, these socioeconomic disparities in health outcomes do not operate independent of race. Race continues to be key in determining social structural factors (e.g., education, income, and occupation), which are also important in explaining racial health disparities.

Second, racial discrimination has been posited as a key explanation in the relationship between race and health among Blacks in the United States. Racial prejudice and discrimination give rise to differences in socioeconomic power (Fiscella & Williams, 2004), residential segregation (Massey, 2004), educational opportunity (Farkas, 2003), and quality and quantity of health care (Casagrande et al., 2007). Various pathways have been identified to explain the relationship between perceived discrimination and health disadvantage. The first pathway suggests that the harmful health effects of discrimination results from the repeated exposure to stress (Mays, Cochran, & Barnes, 2007). Cumulative stressful experiences set in motion a physiological response that may include elevated blood pressure and heart rate, the production of biochemical reaction, and a hypervigilance that may eventually lead to disease and mortality (Mays et al., 2007; Jackson, Williams, & Torres, n.d.). Black men are overrepresented in a broad range of stigmatizing and stressful conditions, including incarceration, homelessness, and unemployment. These conditions may lead to a deterioration in well-being as well as exacerbate the presence of physical and mental illness. A second pathway in which racial discrimination may influence health involves the internalization of negative messages or stereotypes. Discriminatory messages may generate psychic distress, including depression, anxiety, or hostility, as well as a poorer self-evaluation. Such experiences may foster feelings of hopelessness and helplessness, which impair physical and psychological functioning and lead to maladaptive coping strategies, including drug and alcohol use (Jackson et al., n.d.). A third pathway suggests discrimination can affect health indirectly, by withholding vital resources such as access to jobs, education, housing, and capital (Fix & Turner, 1999; Kessler, Mickelson, & Williams, 1999). The loss of these societal resources may threaten an individual's social status and jeopardize quality of life (Fix & Turner, 1999).

Third, residential segregation, Williams and Collins argue (2001), is a fundamental cause of racial disparities in health. Residential segregation operates through many social institutions to affect health. One such institution is the educational system. The public school system is neighborhood based. Income and racial segregation lead to schools that are disparate based on income and race, and the quality of these schools and the education provided is subsequently affected. In a cyclical fashion, lower-quality schools and education lead to lower-wage jobs and poorer neighborhoods. This pattern also influences access to quality health care, healthy food choices, and safe, quality neighborhoods. For example, poorer neighborhoods tend to have lower-quality foods at higher costs than in more affluent areas. William and Collins (2001) found that Blacks pay more for housing, food, and insurance than Whites, which leads to poorer nutrition for Blacks (i.e., poor health) when compared to Whites at the same income levels.

Lastly, mistrust remains a salient barrier among Black Americans in the fight to receive appropriate health treatment, especially mental illness. Mistrust among Blacks stems from both the historical exploitation of Blacks by the medical establishment and continued differential treatment among races/ethnicities by medical personal (Clark, Anderson, Clark, & Williams., 1999). A survey found that 12% of African Americans felt a doctor or health professional judged them unfairly or treated them with disrespect due to their race or ethnicity, as compared with only 1% of Whites (Brown, Shear, Schulberg, & Madonia, 1999). However, other nationally representative surveys of Black Americans found these self-reported incidents of mistreatment by medical professionals to be much higher (LaVeist, Diala, & Jarrett, 2000; Satcher, 2001). There is additional research which suggests that mistrust may be especially pronounced among new immigrants, especially those migrating from countries where government corruption is normative (Satcher, 2001). However, little research has been done examining the role of mistrust and stigma among Black immigrants. Addressing Black mistrust in the medical profession will be salient issue in narrowing racial health disparities.

CONCLUSION

Socioeconomic status (SES) and other resources explain a large portion of racial disparities in health and mortality. However, it is the socially constructed meaning of race that is the cause of the SES and resource inequality by race. For Black men, the impact on health has been traumatic in its scope. Across the life course, except in the oldest age bracket, Black men experience the highest rates of disease, mortality, and lower psychosocial well-being in the United States. Looking at the intersection of race, gender, and nativity, we observe that U.S.-born Black men experience the worst health outcomes of all.

The health of Black men should be deemed a public health emergency. Black men live significantly shorter lives and are disproportionately afflicted with disease, both infectious and chronic. The cumulative effects of stress because of racial disadvantage, both directly and indirectly, are costly for Black men. That is, it costs them in the number of years lived and in quality of life. Though the literature shows that Black women are also at a health disadvantage, the intersection of race, gender, and nativity cannot be ignored.

This chapter discussed substantive issues related to Black male physical and mental health. In addition, we conducted new analyses of adult Black male physical and mental health using two datasets by nativity status. These new analyses reveal several key findings. First, U.S.-born Black men experience worse health, both physical and mental health, across the life course relative to foreign-born Black men. Though this result is unsurprising, it is important to note that the relationship between health and nativity among Black men is not constant across the life course. It converges at older ages for some illnesses such as heart disease and cancer; diverges for some, including SRH; and yet, remains stagnant across the life course for obesity. When examining mental health, we found significant differences in mental health by nativity. U.S.-born Black men, on average, exhibited lower levels of self-mastery, but higher levels of life satisfaction and self-esteem than foreign-born Black men, even after controlling for income, education, and marital status.

Overall, Black men, particularly native born, are at a disadvantage in the United States relative to other racial/ethnic and gender groups, and these disparate health outcomes are persistent across the life course. The social, economic, and political conditions under which Black men exist in the United States have significant and adverse effects on their health and well-being. It has been the focus of continual public health campaigns and is a critical component of the federal government–led initiative Healthy People 2020. There have been modest signs of closing the racial disparity in health, but the gap remains wide. One directive to aid in the closing of this gap in health would be to understand the intersection of race, gender, and nativity to identify the most at-risk and vulnerable populations.

NOTE

1. In this chapter we use the term "Black" to refer to an individual's racial identity, and the term "African American" is used to remain consistent with prior work cited.

REFERENCES

Adams, P. (2003). Understanding the high self-esteem of Black adolescent girls. *Dissertation Abstracts International*, 64(06), (UMI No. 3095496).

Arias, E. (2012). United States life tables. *National Vital Statistics Reports, 61*(3), Division of Vital Statistics.

Bandura, A. (1997). *Self-efficacy: The exercise of control.* New York, NY: Freeman.

Bratter, J. L., & Eschbach, K. (2005). Race/ethnic differences in nonspecific psychological distress: Evidence from the National Health Interview Survey (NHIS). *Social Science Quarterly, 86,* 620–644.

Braveman, P., & Barclay, C. (2009). Health disparities beginning in childhood: A life-course perspective. *Pediatrics, 124*(3), S163–S175.

Brown, C., Shear, M. K., Schulberg, H. C., & Madonia, M. J. (1999). Anxiety disorders among African-American and White primary medical care patients. *Psychiatric Services, 50,* 407–409.

Bruce, M. A., & Thornton, M. C. (2004). It's my world? Exploring Black and White perceptions of personal control. *Sociological Quarterly, 45,* 597–612.

Buchanan, T., & Selmon, N. (2008). Race and gender differences in self-efficacy: Assessing the role of gender role attitudes and family background. *Sex Roles, 58,* 822–836.

Buchanan, T., & Gossett, J. (2002). The healthy homeless minority. *Journal of Social Distress and the Homeless, 12*, 173–204.

Carr, D., Crosnoe, R., Hughes, M. E., & Pienta, A. (Eds.). (2008). *Encyclopedia of the life course and human development* (Vol. 1, pp. 262–268). New York, NY: Macmillan Reference USA.

Casagrande, S. S., Gray, T. L., LaVeist, T. A., Gaskin, D. J., & Cooper, L. A. (2007). Perceived discrimination and adherence to medical care in a radically integrated community. *Journal of General Internal Medicine, 22*, 389–395.

Centers for Disease Control and Prevention (CDC). (2002). Unrecognized HIV infection, risk behaviors, and perceptions of risk among young Black men who have sex with men—six U.S. cities, 1994–1998. *Morbidity and Mortality Weekly Report, 51*, 733–736.

———. (2010) Body mass index: Considerations for practitioners. Retrieved from: http://www.cdc.gov/obesity/downloads/BMIforPactitioners.pdf

———.(2012). Estimated HIV incidence among adults and adolescents in the United States, 2007–2010. *HIV Surveillance Supplemental Report.* http://www.cdc.gov/hiv/library/reports/surveillance/index.html

Clark, R., Anderson, N. B., Clark, V. R., & Williams, D. R. (1999). Racism as a stressor for African Americans. *American Psychologist, 54*, 805–816.

Coale, A. J., & Kisker, E. E. (1986). Mortality crossovers: Reality or bad data? *Population Studies, 40*, 389–401.

Cohen, C. I., Berment, F., & Magai, C. (1997). A comparison of U.S.-born African-American and African-Caribbean psychiatric outpatients. *Journal of the National Medical Association, 89*(2), 117.

Courtenay, W. H. (2000). Constructions of masculinity and their influence on men's well-being: A theory of gender and health. *Social Science & Medicine, 50*(10), 1385–1401.

Doyle, O., Joe, S., & Caldwell, C. H. (2012). Ethnic differences in mental illness and mental health service use among Black fathers. *American Journal of Public Health, 102*(S2) S222-231.

Drevenstedt, G. L., Crimmins, E. M., Vasunilashorn, S., & Finch, C. E. (2008). The rise and fall of excess male infant mortality. *Proceedings of the National Academy of Sciences of the United States, 105*(13), 5016–5021.

Dukes, R. L., & Martinez, R. (1994). The impact of gender on self-esteem among adolescents. *Adolescence, 29*, 105–115.

Emslie, G. J., Weinberg, W. A., Rush, A. J., Adams, R. M., & Rintelmann, J. W. (1990). Depressive symptoms by self-report in adolescence: Phase 1 of the development of a questionnaire for depression by self-report. *Journal of Child Neurology, 5*, 114–121.

Farkas, G. (2003). Racial disparities and discrimination in education: What do we know, how do we know it, and what do we need to know? *Teachers College Record, 105*(6), 1119–1146.

Fiscella, K., & Williams, D. R. (2004). Health disparities based on socioeconomic inequalities: Implications for urban health care. *Academic Medicine, 79*, 1139–1147.

Fix, M. E., & Turner, M. A. (Eds.). (1999). *National report card on discrimination in America.* Washington, DC: Urban Institute.

Fletcher, J. M. (2010). Adolescent depression and educational attainment: Results using sibling fixed effects. *Health Economics, 19*, 855–871.

Frisbie, W. P. (2005). Infant mortality. In D. L. Poston & M. Micklin (Eds.), *Handbook of population* (pp. 251–282). New York, NY: Springer Publishers.

Frisbie, W. P., Hummer, R. A., & McKinnon, S. (2009). Infant and child mortality. In D. Carr, R. Crosnoe, M.E. Hughes, & A. Pienta (Eds.), *Encyclopedia of the life course and human development* (Vol. 1, pp. 262-268). New York, NY: Macmillan.

Gibbs, T. A., Okuda, M., Oquendo, M. A., Lawson, W. B., Wang, S., Thomas, Y. F., & Blanco, C. (2013). Mental Health of African Americans and Caribbean Blacks in the United States: Results from the National Epidemiological Survey on Alcohol and Related Conditions. *American Journal of Public Health, 103*(2), 330–338.

Gray-Little, B., & Hafdahl, A. (2000). Factors influencing racial comparisons of self-esteem: A quantitative review. *Psychological Bulletin, 126*, 26–54.

Gross, J. J., & John, O. P. (2003). Individual differences in two emotion regulation processes: Implications for affect, relationships and well-being. *Journal of Personality and Social Psychology, 85*, 348–362.

Han H. R., Kim, M. T., Rose L., Dennison C., Bone L., & Hill M. N. (2003). Effects of stressful life events in young Black men with high blood pressure. *Ethnicity & Disease, 16*, 64–70.

Hayward, M., Crimmins, E., Miles, T., & Yang, Y. (2000). The significance of socioeconomic status in explaining the race gap in chronic health conditions. *American Sociological Review, 65*, 910–930.

Hayward, M. D., & Heron, M. (1999). Racial inequality in active life among adult Americans. *Demography, 36(1)*, 77–91.

Hill, H. M., & Madhere, S. (1996). Exposure to community violence and African American children: A multidimensional model of risks and resources. *Journal of Community Psychology, 24*, 26–43.

Hughes, M. E., & Thomas, M. (1998). The continuing significance of race revisited: A study of race, class, and quality of life in America, 1972–1996. *American Sociological Review, 63*, 785–795.

Hummer, R. A., Powers, D. A., Pullum, S. G., Gossman, G. L., & Frisbie, W. P. (2007). Paradox found (again): Infant mortality among the Mexican-origin population in the United States. *Demography, 44*(3), 441–457.

Hummer, R. A., & Chinn, J. J. (2011). Race/Ethnicity and U.S. adult mortality: Progress, prospects, and new analyses. *Du Bois Review, 8(1)*, 5–24.

Jackson, J. S., Neighbors, H. W., Nesse, R. M., Trierweiler, S. J., & Torres, M. (2004a). Methodological innovations in the National Survey of American Life. *International Journal of Methods in Psychiatric Research, 13*, 289–98.

Jackson, J. S., Torres, M., Caldwell, C. H., Neighbors, H. W., Nesse, R. N., Taylor, R. J., Trierweiler, S. J., & Williams, D. R. (2004b). The National Survey of American Life: a study of racial, ethnic and cultural influences on mental disorders and mental health. *International Journal of Methods in Psychiatric Research, 13(4)*, 196–207.

Jackson, J. S., Williams, D. R., & Torres, M. (n.d.) *Perceptions of discrimination, health and mental health: The Social Process.* Unpublished paper. Department of Health Behavior & Health Education, University of Michigan, Ann Arbor, MI.

Jackson-Triche, M. E., Sullivan, J. G., Wells, K. B., Rogers, W., Camp, P., & Mazel, R. (1997). Depression and health-related quality of life in ethnic minorities seeking care in general medical setting. Los Angeles, CA: Research Center on Managed Care for Psychiatric Disorders, UCLA Neuropsychiatric Institute and RAND.

Joe, S., Baser, R. E., Breeden, G., Neighbors, H. W., & Jackson, J. S. (2006). Prevalence of and risk factors for lifetime suicide attempts among Blacks in the United States. *Journal of the American Medical Association, 296*, 2112–2123.

Kaestner, R., Pearson, J. A., Keene, D., & Geronimus, A. T. (2009). Stress, allostatic load, and health of Mexican immigrants. *Social Science Quarterly, 90*(5), 1089–1111.

Kent, M. M. (2007). Immigration and America's Black population. *Population Bulletin, 62(4)*, 1–20.

Kessler, R. C., Berglund, P. A., Zhao, S., Leaf, P. J., Kouzis, A. C., Bruce, M. L., Freidman, R. L., Grosser, R. C., Kennedy, C., Narrow, W. E., Kuehnel, T. G., Laska, E. M., Manderscheid,

R. W., Rosenheck, R. A., Santoni, T. W., & Schneier, M. (1996). The 12-month prevalence and correlates of serious mental illness (SMI) (59-70). In R. W. Manderscheid & M. A. Sonnenschein (Eds.), *Mental health, United States*. Rockville, MD: Center for Mental Health Services.

Kessler, R. C., McGonagle, K. A., Zhao, S., Nelson, C. B., Hughes, M., Eshelman, S., Wittchen, H. U., & Kendler, K. S. (1994). Lifetime and 12-month prevalence of DSM–III–R disorders in the United States. *Archives of General Psychiatry, 51*, 8–19.

Kessler, R. C., Mickelson, K. D., & Williams, D. R. (1999). The prevalence, distribution and mental health correlates of perceived discrimination in the United States. *Journal of Health and Social Behavior, 40*, 208–30.

LaVeist, T. A., Diala, C., & Jarrett, N. C. (2000). Social status and perceived discrimination: Who experiences discrimination in the health care system, how, and why? In C. Hogue, M. Hargraves, & K. Scott-Collins (Eds.), *Minority health in America* (pp. 194–208). Baltimore, MD: Johns Hopkins University Press.

Lynch, S. M., Brown, J. S., & Harmsen, K. G. (2003). Black-White differences in mortality compression and deceleration and the mortality crossover reconsidered. *Research on Aging, 25*, 456–483.

Lyons-Ruth, K., Connell, D. B., Grunebaum, H. U., & Botein, S. (1990). Infants at social risk: Maternal depression and family support services as mediators of infant development and security attachment. *Child Development, 61*, 85–98.

Martin, J. A., Hamilton, B. E., Ventura, S. J., Osterman, M. J. K., Wilson, E. C., & Mathews, T. J. (2012). Births: Final data for 2010. *National Vital Statistics Reports, 61*(1), 1–72.

Massey, D. S. (2004). Segregation and stratification: A biosocial perspective. *Du Bois Review, 1*, 7–25.

Masters, R. K. (2012). Uncrossing the U.S. Black-White mortality crossover: The role of cohort forces in life course mortality risk. *Demography, 49*, 773–796.

Mathews, T. J., & MacDorman, M. F. (2012). Infant mortality statistics from the 2008 period linked birth/infant death data set. *National Vital Statistics Reports, 60*(5), 1–28.

Mays, V. M., Cochran, S. D., & Barnes, N. W. (2007). Race, race-based discrimination, and health outcomes among African Americans. *Annual Review of Psychology, 58*, 201–205.

McIntosh, J. L., & Drapeau, C. W. (2012). U.S.A. suicide 2010: Official final data. American Association of Suicidology. Retrieved from http://www.suicidology.org

Mead, G. H. (1934). *Mind, self, and society: From the standpoint of a social behaviorist*. Chicago, IL: The University of Chicago Press.

Millett, G. A., Peterson, J. L., Wolitski, R. J., & Stall, R. (2006). Greater risk for HIV infection of Black men who have sex with men: A critical literature review. *American Journal of Public Health, 96*, 1007–1019.

Mossey, J. M., & Shapiro, E. (1982). Self-rated health: A predictor of mortality among the elderly. *American Journal of Public Health 72*(8), 800–808.

Murphy, S. L., Xu, J. Q., & Kochanek, K. D. (2013). Deaths: Final data for 2010. *National Vital Statistics Reports, 61*(4), 1–118.

Myers, H. F., Lesser, I., Rodriguez, N., Mira, C. B., Hwang, W., Camp, C., Erickson, L., & Wohl, M. (2002). Ethnic differences in clinical presentation of depression in adult women. *Cultural Diversity and Ethnic Minority Psychology, 8*, 138–156.

Nagi, S. Z. (1976). An epidemiology of disability among adults in the United States. *Health and Society, 54*(4), 439–467.

Nam, C. B. (1995). Another look at mortality crossovers. *Social Biology, 42*, 133–142.

Nam, C. B., Weatherby, N. L., & Ockay, K. A. (1978). Causes of death which contribute to the mortality crossover effect. *Biodemography and Social Biology, 25*(4), 306–314.

National Center for Health Statistics. (2013). The National Health Interview Survey (2007–2011), Sample Adult Files. Retrieved from http://www.cdc.gov/nchs/nhis.htm

Palloni, A., & Arias, E. (2004). Paradox Lost: Explaining the Hispanic adult mortality advantage. *Demography, 41*(3), 385–415.

Preston, S. H., & Elo, I. T. (2006). Black mortality at very old ages in official U.S. life tables: A skeptical appraisal. *Population and Development Review, 32*, 557–565.

Read, J. N. G., Emerson, M. O., & Tarlov, A. (2005). Implications of Black immigrant health for U.S. racial disparities in health. *Journal of Immigrant Health, 7*(3), 205–212.

Regier, D. A., Narrow, W. F., Rae, D. S., Manderscheid, R. W., Locke, B. Z, & Goodwin, F. K. (1993). The de facto U.S. mental and addictive disorders service system. Epidemiological and prospective 1-year prevalence rates of disorders and services. *Archives of General Psychiatry, 50*, 85–94.

Rieker, P. P., & Bird, C. E. (2005). Rethinking gender differences in health: Why we need to integrate social and biological perspectives [Special Issue II]. *Journals of Gerontology, 60* (B), 40–47.

Robins, L., & Regier, D. A. (1991). *Psychiatric disorders in America: The epidemiologic catchment area study.* New York, NY: The Free Press.

Rosenberg, M. (1986). *Conceiving the self.* Malabar, FL: Robert E. Krieger Publishing Company.

Rotheram-Boris, M. J., Dopkins, S., Sabate, N., & Lightfoot, M. (1996). Personal and ethnic identity, values and self-esteem among Black and Latino adolescent girls. In B. J. Leadbeater & N. Way (Eds.), *Urban girls: Resisting stereotypes, creating identities* (pp. 35–52). New York, NY: New York University Press.

Ruiz J., Facer, M., & Sun, R. K. (1998). Risk factors for human immunodeficiency virus infection and unprotected anal intercourse among young men who have sex with men. *Sexually Transmitted Disease, 25,* 100–107.

Satcher, D. (2001). *Mental Health: Culture, Race, and Ethnicity—A Supplement to Mental Health: A Report of the Surgeon General.* Washington, DC: U.S. Department of Health and Human Services.

Service, S. K., & Blower, S. M. (1995). HIV transmission in sexual networks: an empirical analysis. *Proceedings Biology Science, 260,* 237–244.

Shaw, B., & Krause, N. (2001). Exploring race variations in aging and personal control. *Journal of Gerontology: Social Sciences, 56B* (2), S119–S124.

Singh, G. K., Miller, B. A. (2004). Health, life expectancy, and mortality patterns among immigrant populations in the United States. *Canadian Journal of Public Health, 3,* 14–21.

Teplin, L. A. (1990). The prevalence of severe mental disorder among male urban jail detainees: Comparison with the Epidemiologic Catchment Area Program. *American Journal of Public Health, 80,* 663–669.

Twenge, J., & Crocker, J. (2002). Race and self-esteem: Meta-analyses comparing Whites, Blacks, Hispanics, Asians, and American Indians and comment on Gray-Little and Hafdahl (2000). *Psychological Bulletin, 128,* 371–408.

U.S. Department of Health and Human Services. (2001). *Mental Health: Culture, Race, and Ethnicity—A Supplement to Mental Health: A Report of the Surgeon General.* Retrieved from http://www.ncbi.nlm.nih.gov/books/NBK44243/

U.S. Department of Health and Human Services. (2006). Health, United States, 2006. U.S. Department of Health & Human Services. Retrieved from www.cdc.gov/nchs/data/hus/hus06.pdf

Verbrugge, L. M., & Jette, A. M. (1994). The disablement process. *Social Science and Medicine, 38*(1), 1–14.

Wade, T. J., Thompson, V., Tashakkori, A., & Valente, E. (1989). A longitudinal analysis of sex by race differences in predictors of adolescent self-esteem. *Personality and Individual Differences, 10*, 717–729.

Waldron, I. (1976). Why do women live longer than men? *Journal of Human Stress, 2*, 2–13.

Walker, S. N., Volkan, K., Sechrist, K. R., & Pender, N. J., (1988). Health promoting life-styles of older adults: Comparisons with young and middle-aged adults, correlates and patterns. *Advances in Nursing Science, 11*, 76–90.

Watkins, D. C., Walker, R. L., & Griffith, D. M. (2009). A meta-study of Black male mental health and well-being. *Journal of Black Psychology, 36*, 303–330.

Wilcox, A., & Russell, I. (1990). Why small Black infants have a lower mortality rate than small White infants: the case for population-specific standards for birth weight. *The Journal of Pediatrics, 116*(1), 7–10.

Williams, D. R. (1996). Race and health: Basic questions, emerging directions. *Annals of Epidemiology, 7*, 322–333.

Williams, D. R., & Collins, C. (2001). Racial residential segregation: A fundamental cause of racial disparities in health. *Public Health Reports, 116*, 404–416.

Williams, D. R., & Jackson, J. S. (2000). Race/ethnicity and the 2000 census: Recommendations for African American and other Black populations in the United States. *American Journal of Public Health, 90*, 1728–1730.

Williams, D. R. (2003). The health of men: Structured inequalities and opportunities. *American Journal of Public Health, 93*, 724-731.

Williams, D. R., & Earl, T. R. (2007). Commentary: Race and mental health—more questions than answers. *International Journal of Epidemiology, 36*, 768–760.

Williams, D. R., Gonzalez, H. M., Neighbors, H., Nesse, R., Abelson, J. M., Sweetman, J., et al. (2007). Prevalence and distribution of major depressive disorder in African Americans, Caribbean Blacks, and Non-Hispanic Whites. *Archives of General Psychiatry, 64*, 305–315.

World Health Organization (WHO). 1946. *Constitution of the World Health Organization.* International Health Conference, New York.

Zhang, A. Y., & Snowden, L. R. (1999). Ethnic characteristics of mental disorders in five U.S. communities. *Cultural Diversity & Ethnic Minority Psychology, 5*(2): 132–146.

CHAPTER SIX

Everyday Struggle: Critical Race Theory and Black Male Doctoral Student Experience

C. SPENCER PLATT

Although Black males receive a great deal of attention in the popular media, much of it is negative, as images of drug dealers, gangsters, players, "baby boys," and underachievers dominate the dialogue. For many, these depictions of Black men shape their entire understanding of the lives and lifestyles of Black men. However, this chapter will examine the experiences of Black male doctoral students (BMDS), a group that seldom receives attention in the popular media and does not receive much more attention in the academic literature. Nonetheless, it is important to examine the experiences of Black male doctoral students with regard to masculinity because it expands our conception of what it means to be a Black male in important ways: 1) they are a model of academic achievement and success as highly educated students en route to earning the highest academic degree available; 2) this chapter underscores the challenges these students encounter with regard to maintaining their cultural identity; and 3) understanding the experiences of BMDS at a predominantly White research university may provide insight on how students of color may be able to navigate their educational experiences at earlier educational levels.

LITERATURE REVIEW

Black Males in Schools

Black students rank at or near the bottom on nearly every quantifiable measure of scholastic achievement in grade school, high school, and in college (Feagin & Sikes, 1995; Jencks & Phillips, 1998; Tierney, 1999; Porter, 2006; Harris, 2006; Cuyjet, 2006). Measures include grade point average, graduation rates, college-going rates, and standardized test scores. These differences are even more striking when broken down by gender as Black male students are lagging behind their Black female counterparts. For example, while female undergraduates typically outnumber male undergraduates across races, the disparity between Black females and Black males is even more pronounced (National Center for Education Statistics [NCES], 2014; Kaba, 2005). Michael Cuyjet (2006) proclaims that Blacks have the most skewed male/female ratios in higher education with women nearly outnumbering men by a 2:1 margin. In 2011–12, Black females earned 7,632 doctoral degrees while Black males earned 4,108, or nearly doubling the number of doctoral degrees earned (NCES, 2014). To be sure, the problems regarding the educational attainment of Black males should not be framed in a way to suggest that Black males are not achieving because Black females crowd them out. Nonetheless, these staggering statistics have long-term consequences for Black males, including lower lifetime earnings, poorer health prospects, shorter life expectancy, and increased risk of imprisonment (Cashin, 2004; Kaba, 2005).

Outside of the achievement gap's obvious socioeconomic consequences for Black males, the educational experience of Black males is important to explore because although higher education clearly provides benefits for individuals, society also benefits and profits from individuals attaining higher education (and, by extension, doctoral degrees). College graduates have lower unemployment rates and less reliance on government assistance programs like welfare and unemployment, they commit fewer crimes, and they help form a generally better educated citizenry (Perna, 2000; Cashin, 2004). Individual citizens benefit, society benefits, and institutions of higher education and their entire student population reap educational benefits by increasing their diversity (Hurtado, 1992; *Grutter v. Bollinger*, 2003). Furthermore, public institutions of higher education generally have a charge and expectation to serve the residents of their respective states, not only through undergraduate education, but also in graduate and professional school education as well. It is essential that the duty to serve residents of the state continues to extend to communities of color. It is equally as important to have a diverse body of doctoral students who represent leadership and the future within various fields and sectors.

Black Doctoral Recipients

According to the National Center for Educational Statistics (2014), in 2011–12, of the 170,062 doctoral degrees conferred 109,270 went to Whites, 17,893 went to Asians, 11, 740 went to Blacks and 9,215 went to Hispanics. Against this backdrop, in 2004, according to the *Journal of Blacks in Higher Education* (2006b), Blacks earned a record number of doctoral degrees. That year's total of 1,879 doctoral degrees earned by Blacks was 7.1% of total doctoral degrees earned. This number was a sharp increase from the 1987 total of 787 doctorates earned by Blacks. However, it is important to note that despite the fact that Blacks have been earning more doctorates (Blacks earned 70% more doctorates in 2000 than in 1977), Black women are far outpacing Black men (Nettles & Millett, 2006). In 1981, Black males earned 54.9% of doctorates awarded to Blacks, but by 2000, the share had dropped to 38.8% (Nettles and Millett, 2006).

In doctoral programs, like previous stages of the educational pipeline, Blacks appear to lag behind other racial and ethnic groups in most indicators of success. Black doctoral students are presenting less at conferences, graduate with fewer scholarly publications, and lag in timely progress toward the degree (Nettles & Millett, 2006). Why are the best and brightest underrepresented students lagging behind Whites and Asians at the doctoral level? Nettles and Millett found that Black and Latino graduate students were more likely to obtain fellowships, but less likely to receive assistantships than White students. Blacks were less likely to have mentors in math and the sciences (Nettles, 1989; Nettles & Millet, 2006). Moreover, Black students were also less likely to be mentored by the more productive faculty or faculty who publish, teach, secure funding, and perform service (Nettles & Millett, 2006). In Nettles and Millett's (2006) national study of over 9,000 graduate students at 21 universities, no field graduated even 50% of its Black doctoral students. This finding strongly suggests differences in the socialization of Black students.

Nettles and Millett (2006) posit that the lower GRE scores of Black students may keep them from working with the best and most productive faculty as these faculty members desire to work with the most highly regarded graduate students. However, the GRE, much like the SAT at the undergraduate level, serves as a gatekeeper of access to higher education. Students of color and low-income students routinely score significantly lower on these tests than middle-class White and Asian counterparts. Standardized test scores are accepted uncritically to represent objective measures of student intelligence, hard work, and preparation. In actuality, they may be more accurate in reflecting structural issues in educational systems and segregated neighborhoods. It is no secret that students that hail from families with high incomes and high levels of educational attainment perform better on standardized tests than others (Bowen, Kurzweil & Tobin, 2005). Bowen,

Kurzweil and Tobin (2005) found that over 20% of students from the top income quartile scored over 1200 on the SAT compared to just 7% from the lowest income quartile, but one-third of the racial gap in test scores are accounted for by differences in family income and parental education with the other two-thirds explained by other measures of family circumstances such as grandparents' education, the quality of the mother's schooling, and household size.

Doctoral Students and Academic Socialization

Weidman, Twale, and Stein (2001) have created a theory of graduate student professional socialization based largely on Thornton and Nardi's (1975) framework for role acquisition and Weidman's (1989) theory of socialization for undergraduate students. The theory of graduate student socialization borrowed the four stages of Thornton and Nardi's role acquisition theory: anticipatory, formal, informal, and personal stages. Weidman's (1989) theory of undergraduate socialization aids the theory of graduate student socialization as it lends an emphasis on interaction and norms. These are particularly important to the socialization of students as interaction refers to social interaction between faculty and students and norms "represent generalized conceptions of what constitutes appropriate behavior" (Weidman, 1989, p. 49). The academic department serves as a normative reference point through interaction with both faculty and student peers.

An important aspect of socialization is the process of receiving the norms, values, traditions, expectations, and ideologies of a particular group. Socialization is conceptualized as a stage theory with two important features: it is a developmental process and core elements—such as knowledge acquisition, investment, and involvement—are associated with development of role identity and commitment (Stein, 1992; Thornton & Nardi, 1975; Weidman et al., 2001). Gardner (2008) explains that socialization "affects every part of the student experience from the first contact with a graduate program through the dissertation defense" (p. 129). Socialization is key in doctoral persistence. Those who have a successful socialization are more likely to persist to graduation, while by contrast, those who have a less successful socialization processes are at an increased likelihood of dropping out. Equally important is the fact that although graduate student socialization is a stage theory, it is not linear, but rather fluid and interactive (Weidman & Stein, 2003).

On one level, they are being socialized into the graduate student experience and through this they learn how to survive and eventually thrive as graduate students. However, on another level, they are also learning to be academics as they are initiated into the cultures of both their field and their institution. Doctoral programs can be seen as the anticipatory stage of academic careers.

It is in graduate school that doctoral students are introduced to the roles and expectations of academia by faculty and advisors. Interaction with faculty and advisors play a key role in the socialization of doctoral students. In Nettles and Millet's 2006 study of 9,036 doctoral students, they found that academic interaction with faculty was an area where race and discipline mattered. Blacks and Hispanics reported different experiences in doctoral programs than their White colleagues. Blacks and Hispanics were found to be less likely to graduate, and less likely to have strong faculty mentors aid in the development. These findings clearly indicate that more research is needed on the experiences of Black males in doctoral programs in order to ascertain the root causes of and possible solutions to this stark disparity between White and minority doctoral students.

Doctoral student socialization activities and experiences are often those that both acquaint them with their formal roles and responsibilities, as well as the hidden expectations of their advisors, department, and university. This includes activities and experiences that aid in their development as a future faculty members and professionals. Some of the activities and experiences are interactions with faculty, peer interactions, faculty mentorship, research and publishing, fellowships, teaching assistantships, and research assistantships (Gardner 2007; Golde, 1998; Nettles & Millett, 2006; Weidman et al., 2001). Weidman and company argue that success is predicated not only on successful management and completion of academic demands, but also on student ability to recognize many of the informal and subtle attitudes, values, and politics of faculty and peers in their program (Weidman et al., 2001). It is through the socialization process that students acquire not only their new roles but also the values, attitudes, interests, skill, knowledge, and culture of the group they are earning admission into (Merton, Reader & Kendall, 1957).

METHODOLOGY

This study explores the experiences of Black male doctoral students through individual interviews using a semi-structured protocol. Interviews were audio recorded, transcribed verbatim, coded, and analyzed. Individual interviews were the primary mode of investigating this phenomenological study. The overarching goal of the study was to increase understanding of what it is like to be a Black male doctoral student at a large PWI, what some of the experiential commonalities between Black men in doctoral programs are, and where they find sources of support.

Advantages of qualitative work include the ability to study individuals in their setting and to give voice to the marginalized. The in-depth interview is the favored "digging tool" for the social scientist (Benny and Hughes, 1970). The strengths of in-depth interviewing are its flexibility and dynamic qualities (Taylor and Bogden, 1998). It is a tool directed toward learning about knowledge and attitudes that cannot be observed easily or directly.

Participants were identified through department chairpersons and graduate coordinators. The Black Graduate Student Association and African/African American Studies listservs were also utilized to identify participants. Individual semi-structured interviews took between 90 and 120 minutes each. Each participant was interviewed twice and took part in additional follow-up interviews as needed. Interview topics included experiences in the doctoral programs, sources of support, professional and cognitive socialization, institutional and departmental culture, time management, and doctoral persistence and attrition. Students were asked to fill out a brief survey on demographic and descriptive information.

All of the participants in this study were Black males who were enrolled and in good standing with a doctoral program. Participants came from a wide variety of fields and disciplines. Homogenous sampling methods were employed to interview individuals based on membership in a subgroup that has distinct characteristics (Creswell, 2005), but the participants varied widely in terms of background characteristics apart from racial categorization. Participants were identified through criterion sampling (Creswell, 1998; Patton, 2002), specifically:

1. Are pursuing a Ph.D. (not other doctorates).
2. Are enrolled in their third year of doctoral study or beyond.
3. Are full-time students.
4. Entered their Ph.D. programs with aspirations to become university researchers.

Data Collection and the Interview Process

Nine Black male doctoral students agreed to participate in two in-depth, face-to-face interviews and follow-up interviews via telephone (Harper, 2008). However, several participants were living and conducting research in other parts of the country; for those participants interviews were conducted via telephone.

Participants in the study completed a profile, which included background information on home and family structures prior to the doctoral program, their current home situation, socioeconomic status, educational history, relationship status, and organizational affiliations. Pseudonyms are used to protect the anonymity of all participants (Taylor & Bogdan, 1998). There is a very limited population of Black male doctoral students at this institution, despite the fact that it is one of the largest research universities in the United States; therefore, degree areas will be clustered when discussing results to preserve the anonymity of participants. Clarification and member checking (Lincoln & Guba, 1986) was done through follow-up meetings and phone calls with individual participants, as well as meetings with small groups of participants.

Lincoln and Guba (1986) prescribe credibility, transferability, dependability, and confirmability to ensure methodological and procedural rigor for qualitative studies. The following measures were taken to ensure the trustworthiness, credibility, dependability, transferability, and confirmability of this study: informal observations, follow-up interviews, peered briefings, and member checking. To ensure credibility, feedback was solicited from faculty and doctoral students who are experienced qualitative researchers and are familiar with Black men's issues or with doctoral student issues. Peer debriefing, or "exposing oneself to a disinterested peer in a manner paralleling an analytic session and for the purpose of exploring aspects of the inquiry that might otherwise remain only implicit within the inquirer's mind," was utilized (Denzin & Lincoln, 2000, p. 308).

Data Analysis Procedures

Each interview was audio taped and transcribed for analysis. Analysis through the constant comparative method (Bogdan & Biklen, 2003) in conjunction with the doctoral socialization (Weidman et al, 2001) and Critical Race Theory conceptual frameworks resulted in a series of codes, which were then compiled into a larger set of themes. Once interviews were imported, each transcript was read twice before an attempt to identify important themes and establish categories was made. In this method, known as eyeballing, the data is handled multiple times before the researcher imposes beliefs and assumptions on the data. Through this exercise, I have gained a better understanding of the respondents' perspectives. In the third round of reading, I began data analysis by looking for word repetition, key terms, and key words in context. This emergent process has allowed for themes and constructs to be incorporated as the analysis of the interview data progresses.

Disclosure of Personal Interest-Positionality

The researcher was at the time a Black male doctoral student, member of the executive boards of both a campus and a national organization that advocates for Black graduate students. Although I currently serve as a Black faculty member, at the time of interviewing I was an insider in many ways.

Participants

The study examines the experiences of nine Black male doctoral students. They hail from all different walks of life. This section serves to give a brief introduction to each participant while highlighting a few essential aspects of their journeys.

Jamaal

Jamaal is from an urban area in the Mid-Atlantic region of the United States. His doctoral studies were in a Liberal Arts degree field. He comes from a middle-class, college-educated, two-parent household with one older male sibling. With regard to education, he feels that he had largely been relegated to the margins of two societies as a Black honors student in virtually all-White classes throughout high school:

> I had 12 years of perfect attendance and I was in honors classes. You know what the honors system always does, it divides. You know how that goes, "you are acting White," whatever, whatever. It put me into a White social circle, but I am still living in a Black neighborhood. Still, I never had the type of, "the Black kids don't accept me" experience, but I was like it is what it is and keep it moving.

Jamaal expressed that as a Black honors student in the Northeast, he learned at an early age how much the perspectives and life experiences of the Black community in which he lived differed from that of elite Whites.

In college, Jamaal was so frustrated with his educational experiences that he contemplated not only leaving the university, but leaving the country. "At the end of my freshman year I was like, 'I can't stand America I got to leave' and I really considered dropping out of school, but friends talked me out of it." Later in his undergraduate experience, fueled by his racial frustration, Jamaal found opportunities to study abroad in Kenya, Ghana, Columbia, and Cuba. In the midst of these travels and studies, he found the desire to continue his education into the doctoral degree.

Melvin

Melvin is a student from the West Coast. At the time of the study, he was earning his doctorate in a program within the College of Communications. He is from a single-parent household, raised by his mother. However, Melvin's father was present throughout his life, even after his parents divorced when he was ten years old.

High school and college were very challenging times for Melvin. The difficulties were experienced partly because he felt isolated and marginalized as one of the few Black students in both educational settings, but also because of problems in his family. Academics were his escape. For long periods of his life, it was one of the few ways he knew how to deal with racism and a difficult home life:

> It was tough because I didn't prepare myself to have to prove myself all over again as a Black student, not just to the faculty, but also to the fellow students who were all thinking "Ok he's here because he's Black," so it was tough getting through undergrad. I was depressed quite a bit, for a while I got to the point where I didn't even care if I lived or died. I stopped going to classes, I stopped eating, for about a year and a half it was really dark. Part of it was school and part of it was family life as my dad went from being an alcoholic to being a hardcore drug user. Seeing that deterioration in him going from a functioning alcoholic to completely dysfunctional and seeing my mom still suffering through some things and financially not knowing where she is going to be living.

Through all of this Melvin was able to maintain a competitive grade point average. He suggests that he was able to do this largely because he found solace in academics. Even when he almost stopped caring whether he lived or died, he still cared about academics enough to persist.

Peter

Peter is also from the West Coast of the United States. His parents have both earned college degrees and remain married to one another. His family moved away from a Black neighborhood after there was an increase in violent crimes. Peter spent the remainder of his youth growing up in a predominantly White community where he felt he was an outsider both in the neighborhood as well as in the school system:

> My family is actually a very academic family, my mother, father, and both of my sisters went to and graduated from [Competitive Universities], but I was the 'White sheep' of the family. I was trying to catch up to the scholastic achievements that my parents and sisters made.

Although he did gain access to a similar top-tier school, there was never much doubt that Peter would go to college. It is ironic that the family's underachiever, the 'White sheep' of the family, ultimately became the one to pursue his doctorate. Difficulties encountered in grade school and high school equipped Peter with the mental fortitude and will to persist that he feels gave him a great advantage during college and graduate school. In high school he struggled significantly, but he learned how to think critically and deal with isolation and marginalization. This served him well when he went to college: as other students were struggling with trying to figure out how to deal with adjusting to the PWI environment, he was able to concentrate on academics. This allowed him to get off to a strong start and gain confidence in academics in ways that he had never known. From there he was able to excel.

Corey

Corey, from a small town in Texas, is a doctoral student in education and is married with children. His parents remain married to one another; both have earned associates degrees. Corey has always been highly involved in student government and as a graduate student he has served in several leadership capacities on campus. His involvement is partly due to a passion for improving the student experience, but also because he feels that as a Black male, he needs every angle and every advantage possible:

> I believe that I have to do as much as I can, but if I put all of my eggs into the basket of being an academic and that doesn't happen, I won't have anything to fall back on. I have also felt that I have to do all of these things because it puts me on an even playing field. Say that there was this person looking to be an academic and he has published three articles, applying for the same position and I have published three articles, I have always felt that the thing that gave me an edge and that offset my color was the extra thing that I did. I have always believed that people see my color as a disadvantage so the three published articles doesn't look as good from me as it does from the White male.

Despite the messages Corey has received from faculty regarding how to acquire an academic post after graduation, his long-held views on race in America convinced him that as a Black male he has to do twice the work if he is to ever get ahead. Although he aspires to a faculty role, he feels that he must gain the type of experiences that make him marketable outside of academe. Despite messages he receives primarily from White faculty and White graduate student peers that "he is a Black male, he will be ok," experience and history send him a different message. He feels that he must be "twice as good, just to be seen as equal."

Table 1: Descriptions of Respondents.

Name	Neighborhood	K-12 Schooling	Traditional Doctoral Student	College	Marital Status	Children	Region
Cedric	Diverse	Diverse	No	College of Education	Single	No	South Atlantic
Corey	Black	Diverse	No	College of Education	Married	Yes	WSC
Earnest	Diverse	Diverse	No	College of Education	Married	Yes	WSC
Elijah	Black	PWS	No	Liberal Arts	Single	No	WSC
Jamaal	Black	PWS	Yes	Liberal Arts	Single	No	Mid-Atlantic

Name	Neighborhood	K-12 Schooling	Traditional Doctoral Student	College	Marital Status	Children	Region
Melvin	White	PWS	No	College of Communications	Domestic Partnership	No	Pacific
Peter	White	PWS	Yes	College of Communications	Single	No	South Atlantic
Reggie	Black	PWS	No	College of Education	Married	Yes	Pacific
Terrence	White	PWS	No	College of Education	Married	No	Pacific

Notes:
PWS=Predominantly White k-12 school(s)
Neighborhood: neighborhood(s) during high school years
Pred. White=Predominately white institutions
Official U.S. Regions designated by the Census Bureau
South Atlantic:Delaware, Maryland, District of Columbia, Virginia, West Virginia, North Carolina, South Carolina, Georgia, Florida
Pacific:Alaska, Washington, Oregon, California, Hawaii
WSC=West South Central: Texas, Louisiana, Oklahoma & Arkansas

Reggie

Reggie is an education doctoral student from an urban area in the South Atlantic region of the United States. He was the youngest of three children raised by a single-parent mother in low-income, predominantly Black neighborhoods. Reggie is currently married with one child. Reggie's journey to the doctorate is unconventional, having completely fallen through the cracks in K-12 education without ever having his academic talent recognized or discovered:

> I was an average to below-average student; I didn't emphasize schooling or grades. I did just enough so I could stay eligible to play sports in high school. I simply wasn't an outstanding student; in fact, my family probably prayed me through school because I was subject to not making it through school. It wasn't because I was a bad child I just didn't do my work. I don't think it ever really changed until I got out of high school. I graduated from high school with probably a 2.2 grade point average. I never took the ACT, and I never took the SAT in fact, I never even considered college. I got out of high school and got a job at the post office because my brother worked there. I was a seasonal worker at the bulk mail center I made $5.50 an hour unloading trucks before I finally ended up going to trade school.

Reggie's route to the doctorate included jobs at the post office, UPS, and in construction. He also attended trade school and became a heating, ventilation, and air conditioning (HVAC) specialist before going to college. Reggie claimed that his "Damascus road" experience regarding education came as he was on the construction crew standing inside the frame of a high-rise building in December "freezing his butt off" at that point he decided to "give education a try."

Earnest

Earnest is a doctoral student in education. He is married with one child and comes from a two-parent family. Earnest decided to take his wife away from their comfortable life to pursue a doctoral degree for the opportunity to find more fulfilling work. Earnest's route was non-traditional: he worked as an educator for several years and earned a master's degree online. He was contemplating earning his doctorate online when he ran across the name of a Black male faculty member that he had known from another institution and decided to contact him and ask a few questions about the doctoral degree. Leaving their lives in another state behind to pursue his dream of earning a doctoral degree and a new career proved to be challenging. Initially, it was a difficult dream for his wife to accept because she felt that they were already approaching living the "Cosby lifestyle." Both he and his wife were leading productive careers, owned their own home, and were enjoying life. However, Earnest was restless and felt that he could do more with regards to his career. She soon relented and they moved so Earnest could continue his education.

Elijah

Elijah is a doctoral student in the College of Liberal Arts. He is from the West South Central region of the United States. He and his sister were raised by a single mother in an urban, high-poverty, high-minority environment:

> I had to take the bus to school; I didn't go to the same school with all the other folks in the projects. I went to a magnet school. I really feel like your associates can make a difference; birds of a feather flock together. All of my friends from school were going to college, but they weren't living in the projects. I was the only one in the projects. I didn't want to be the one who was not going to college. But on the other hand, at the neighborhood school, nobody was talking about going to college. You have to be a very strong person to say, "No, forget that, I am leaving all of this behind and I am going to college anyway." The peer pressure, the want to be liked, you don't want to stand out like that sometimes. But I was that person to my community to where I never had that peer pressure. I remember in elementary school, a cat said, "Nah he can't play the game with us right now, he got to go do his homework." But he was in the same class that I was in! He wasn't talking about me bad, like I got to go do my homework. He was like, "Elijah brings his books home, he has got

to do his homework and he will be out in a little while." Like he was an older dude trying to look out for me but he was my age.

Elijah and his family did not have much financially, but they did have a passion for learning and education. Elijah also described the support he found in the community even from unexpected sources like his childhood peers. His experiences in this urban, predominantly Black community fostered within him a love for the community and the desire to use his talents to give back.

Cedric

Cedric is a doctoral student in the College of Education. His parents never married, but had joint custody of him, causing him to spend significant chunks of time in two different states. The time spent with his mother was often in low-income, high-minority communities. However, the time spent with his father and paternal grandmother afforded him the opportunity experience the lifestyle of upper-middle class Blacks, like spending summer vacations near Martha's Vineyard. Cedric's family always expected educational excellence from him and he met those expectations by performing at the highest level throughout his education. Cedric recalled:

> In sixth grade, Dad was overseas in Egypt and heard that I made two C's on my report card and grounded me, from Egypt. He was going to make sure I respected his punishment. No television and no games. I couldn't do anything but go to school and come home to study until the next report card.

Receiving "punishment" from his dad, in Egypt, for poor grades made it clear that academic underachievement was not a viable option for him.

Terrence

Terrence is from the West Coast. He is a married doctoral student in the College of Education. His parents remain married to one another. His father is a military veteran who has earned an advanced degree and his mother also has a college degree. He is the younger of their two children. The family moved around the country a bit when he was younger. Terrence's family often lived in predominantly White neighborhoods and attended private, predominantly White schools. Terrence reported that he was always one of the only Black people both in school and the community. However, his parents made concerted efforts to connect him to his African American heritage through the Black church, Black civic organizations, as well as frequent visits to extended family members in other states. He feels that these experiences have enabled him to be a balanced and well-adjusted individual, comfortable in a wide range of settings.

FINDINGS

Challenges of Fitting In and Standing Out

Socialization can, at times, challenge the cultural foundations held by people of color, specifically African Americans and Latinos (Gonzalez, 2006). These cultural foundations are typically regarding family and community. The tension between socialization and cultural foundations is similar to the tension in Vincent Tinto's (1994) theorization of student retention in *Leaving College* where he compares students leaving college to committing suicide. Socialization, from the majority perspective, is necessary for success in academia, which includes adherence to the attitudes, norms, values, and expectations of the department and field of study. According to this perspective, those who fail to become properly socialized into their academic departments and fields will be marginalized and are likely to never earn the doctorate and/or lead unproductive academic careers. William Tierney's (1999) critique of Tinto's theory of student departure added the perspectives and experiences of students of color, who do not view cultural suicide as a viable option; they find alternative routes of success. Similarly, Black male doctoral students find alternative sources of success, diversifying the academy and the academic literature as they go.

Freire (1970) defines prescription as the process by which there is an imposition of oppressor's choices over those of the oppressed for the purpose of transforming the consciousness of the oppressed. Juan Carlos Gonzalez (2006) argues that doctoral socialization can be a form of prescription or acculturation for students of color. For students of color, acculturation—that is, the adopting or borrowing traits of another culture—is considered a danger of higher education socialization as they risk being marginalized and isolated within communities of color in addition to the marginalization they face on campus. For the doctoral student of color, the threat is two-fold, coming from being marginalized on campus by race and of losing their personal/cultural identity.

People of color who lose the ability to connect with the issues of racial minorities and adopt majoritarian perspectives are often accused, particularly by other people of color, of "selling out" or turning their backs on their community. Black male doctoral students and other students of color often guard against and therefore resist socialization that might sever their ties to their racial/ethnic community. However, the culture of their department and field of study can make this a difficult task. In departments and fields that are less open to diverse perspectives, students of color find their cultures experiences, perspectives, and concerns absent in the curriculum or presented from deficit perspectives. This also poses challenges for doctoral students of color as they select research and dissertation topics, particularly when there are few faculty of color or others that may assist them in navigating race in their research.

According to Freire (1970), the oppressed have a clearer vision of reality through their experiences. It is precisely this clearer vision of reality that adds tremendous value to the perspectives of students and faculty of color because they are able to see both perspectives; of the dominant majority, as well as the minority perspectives. Their research is, in turn, often bolstered by the life experiences of seeing from two perspectives.

Elijah explained this challenge facing highly educated people of color: they must keep one foot outside of the academy. He argued that the curriculum is often insufficient for people of color; as a result, they must take it upon themselves to protect themselves from elements of their education that may be reductive or lacking:

> If you never saw yourself in the curriculum, but you accepted that curriculum as something you had to go through to get to the next level, then you are being indoctrinated, you are being miseducated, and the education that you are getting is giving you all kinds of ideas and philosophies that are not of your people's making. You may begin to think, view the world, and live your life as if you have blue eyes. A person, who goes through high school and learns nothing but European stuff, gets through college and gets nothing but European stuff, and then they come to do graduate work with usually a European mindset. Your basis is European unless you got a lot of education outside of the classroom that shifted your worldview.

The Black community is aware of the possibility that socialization could have what they perceive as a negative impact on BMDS. Earnest gave an example that illustrates the pull that family and the Black community exert to keep Black scholars close and grounded:

> I think the biggest things for Black Ph.D.'s and people of color is that we still want to be connected to the community and is kind of perceived that if you do certain things you are not really connected with the community or with your family. When you come back, people are like, "Hey don't think you better than anybody just because you got that education." I'm like, "Dang Mom, I just want a salad I don't want fried chicken today! That's all, I just want a salad." They say, "You went off and now you don't eat meat!" And I am like, "It is not even that deep." So I think sometimes there is this pressure on us to keep it real but at the same time be intelligent.

This example, while humorous, illustrates both the Black scholars desire to remain connected to the family/community and the family/community's intention to hold him accountable to cultural roots and traditions. To Earnest and his mother, this exchange was not solely about whether or not he ate fried chicken at this particular outing. This was also about the family/community support for the Black male doctoral student and desires to see him do well, but not wanting his upward mobility to cause the loss of his culture, values, and connection with them.

Balancing changes that naturally occur over time with academics and socialization can be challenging. Doctoral students of color often find they must resist socialization's efforts to make them what Gonzalez (2006) refers to as "homogenized." Doctoral socialization, in some ways, pressures students of color to minimize important aspects of their background and personality in order to think and perform in line with the norms of academic life.

Earnest spoke about wrestling with the idea of remaining your authentic self while undergoing immense intellectual and academic growth:

> I was just thinking the other day, I don't think it's necessarily that you have to change who you are to be successful academics, but I do think based on what you've learned that your dispositions are going to change naturally because you're in this particular profession. I think people naturally change based on their experiences. I feel like you to get into a Ph.D. program to change because you will be introduced to new things and it is going to affect the way you look at things. But I still think you can still remain true to yourself.

A part of the challenge for students of color attempting to maintain their cultural identity and autonomy from the social norms of the doctoral program is, indeed, the intellectual expansion that must occur when exposed to a wide range of theories and perspectives. This growth is expected and should be embraced. For Black male doctoral students, this is more complicated than simply growing and expanding, as they must consider to what degree they are willing to assimilate or resist assimilation. Peter summed up this challenge well:

> It's not that people are changing (that is wrong), but it's that we aren't recognizing what we are changing into. We are supposed to change, but you are supposed to be aware of what you are changing into. People think it's an unconscious thing, but you control what you change into. You channel what you want to be, but we sometimes let other forces dictate who we are, what we are going to be, and where we are going to go and that should not happen.

Black male doctoral students, like all doctoral students, must assert themselves and their own wills to consciously become the scholars that they hope to become. For example, Corey currently has a Black male advisor who meshes well with his research interests. However, prior to connecting with this Black advisor, he worked with a White professor on a topic that he was not very passionate about. For a while, it was presumed that the White professor would be his advisor because they had a great relationship and were able to publish some of their work. However, Corey was ultimately miserable and dreaded working on their projects. He understood that by choosing the Black professor, he might not graduate as quickly because he will not have a predetermined research agenda, but feels that this is a much better fit for the type of work he would like to do. It is important to note that Corey was fortunate that the Black faculty member was available to chair his committee, as many Black doctoral students do not have the option of having a Black dissertation chairperson.

Walking the Minefield

Doctoral socialization can hinder a student's agency (Gonzalez, 2006) or ability to assertively address his or her own grievances. Doctoral students often feel powerless, with few options and little ability to take a stand. It is not uncommon for doctoral students to work as a teaching assistant or graduate research assistant for their committee chairperson or other influential committee members, which places their academics and their finances under the control of the same person. Corey argued that despite this, doctoral students of color have a responsibility to stand up for themselves, refuse to be marginalized, and demand a full doctoral education from start to finish. However, this may be easier said than done, since students fear that if things go badly, they not only jeopardize their career aspirations, but also their current financial arrangements impacting their ability to pay for basic necessities such as rent and food:

> I think we as students have some responsibility as well, because we're grown-ups. We can speak up when there are issues or concerns because we're spending our money and borrowing money to be here. For example, if you got to McDonalds and they don't give you your fries you are going to go back and ask for your fries because you paid for them. The same thing has to apply to our education. If you see something missing, you have a responsibility to ask for what is missing.

Corey is certainly correct in that doctoral students have some responsibility to advocate for themselves. However, many students do not advocate for themselves effectively; some of the reasons include: 1) Fear of reprisal; 2) feelings of powerlessness; and 3) fear of damaging important relationships with faculty.

Melvin argued that understanding who your allies are is extremely important to Black male doctoral students. He also stressed the value of having more than one ally. He stated:

> The people that I work with really look out for me. If you can find that somewhere, and hopefully it's not just one person because that one person can always up and leave, so look for more than one and it makes all the difference. Having the support of faculty is huge. I have seen two people not be able to get through comps because the faculty members aren't supporting them. It's like some political thing and they don't like the person or their research or how they do their research but it's because the faculty have decided that they were not going to let them through. However, having somebody that's on your side saying, "No, they are going to make it through." It makes a huge difference.

Black male doctoral students must also consider popular imagery of the angry Black male, and their very presence may be considered to be threatening and intimidating to faculty, adding an additional layer of consideration and difficulty when advocating for themselves. While it is certainly true that all doctoral students should learn to advocate for themselves and develop strategic partnerships, it is particularly important for Black male doctoral students, due to the history and legacy of stereotypes of Black males around issues of intelligence, work ethic, violence and sexuality. All of which can make navigating a doctoral degree and advocating for one self more complicated.

Peter offered an illustration that demonstrates how he and others in his field challenged the status quo and created new opportunities for Black scholars:

> Most grad students will tough it out and go along to get along, so they will go to all these classes, conferences, stupid get-togethers at bars and happy hours that they don't want to go to. Most will go to housewarmings and stuff like that with no other Black person in sight, but they still feel like they have to do it. They go to conferences where they don't talk about any Black issues at the conference; not one panel, not one presentation. Since they weren't going to look at our issues and problems and things that we want to do, we decided to start our own organization with our own conference.

Peter has been able to be successful in his defiant posture primarily because he has been able to find alternative sources of support for his doctoral endeavors. He has found funding for his research largely outside of his department, both on campus and in the community. Several others in this study were much more cautious about "ruffling the feathers" of faculty and administrators.

Jamaal felt marginalized within his department. He felt that several faculty members had decided that his ideas were not valuable and dismissed his work. Jamaal stated:

> My biggest challenge has been certain fundamental assumptions that are normed within the department. They are political ideas, political understandings that I don't necessarily share with a lot of the other folks. So my biggest challenge with the few professors has been the dismissal of my work, but there would be no intellectual basis for it; it would be more like an emotional thing like, "Oh you don't agree with my politics" but you are not talking about the ideas. I might intellectually get it if you tell me how my way doesn't work. There is one thing I have come to realize and it really bothers me in many ways; grad school is a lot like professional school, it is not much different than a business program or law program because it teaches you how to become a professor and a lot of the time it is at the expense of intellectual ideas.

Melvin experienced a similar dismissal of his research. While his research was accepted within his department, when he went to conferences he felt that his ideas were not welcomed. He expressed the following:

> One of my biggest challenges has been proving the worth of my research, because in my field you don't talk about race, you don't talk about issues of power; it's about maximizing profits. They are trying to understand difference but without trying to understand the power dynamics behind that difference. When I started going to conferences and I was talking about Black men and later on talking about hegemony and issues like that they were like, but what does this have to do with this field? So it's been a constant struggle for the first three years just to prove the worth of my research. I remember going to a conference in Norway and there were a quite a few professors there from Europe and they thought this is worthless, what is this going to do for us? Maybe this in anthropology or sociology, but this doesn't fit in our field.

Black male doctoral students and other underrepresented doctoral students of color must balance learning the requisite skills, knowledge, and values of socialization with some of the cultural messaging that may occur. Moreover, they must learn not only when, but also how to resist, support, and stand up and speak up. They must figure out how to argue, what arguments are compelling, how interests converge, and leveraging support from vital allies. Some argue that viewing doctoral education through this political lens (Bolman & Deal, 2008) is off-putting and refusal to "play the game." However, this is an important part of being a doctoral student. All doctoral students must grapple with many of these issues to some extent, but Black males in doctoral programs feel as if they are in a very precarious position, having taken the plunge and made the investment in time, resources, and money, but with few allies, they may often feel that they cannot afford the mistakes that others might make.

Nonetheless, Peter argues that Black male doctoral students have an obligation to speak up and stand up, even in the classroom. Peter gives a concrete example of how he stood up and the consequences:

> In class once, they are still around here talking about D. W. Griffith and the aesthetics of *The Birth of a Nation*. They were talking about how great the film is, like they can't see the Black man being portrayed as a savage and talking about lynching and stuff. They say, "Yes there are those racial elements but you can't question the actual"...but I am like, "Yes you can. And I will." They stopped having those discussions around me, but they still feel comfortable doing that around some of the other Black or Mexican women.

Some doctoral students, including Black male doctoral students, would have difficulty in speaking up and expressing that they were offended by the conversation of racial matters and the dismissal of Black people's suffering. Perhaps, it is expected that doctoral students would always express their perspectives. However, this does not always occur since students feel that they must weigh the costs. Another problem with passivity and silence, though, is that it becomes expected and students then unwittingly lose the respect of their faculty and student peers alike. On the other end of the spectrum, Black male doctoral students and other students of color feel they must often be the spokesperson for their race and culture, perhaps garnering no more respect from White faculty and students than their silenced Black and Latino counterparts.

Doctoral students sometimes "play the game" or perform whatever role is expected of them. At what point can those who have chosen to play the game be their authentic selves? Does this take place after they leave campus, after obtaining a faculty post, on weekends, or after earning tenure? Is a scholar at some point able to hit reset and become outspoken after spending years biding time and biting his tongue? The larger question is, can the game be played with integrity and self-respect? Being wise regarding when and where to express your true feelings is not in and of itself playing the game. For the Black male doctoral students in this study, many of their mentors and role models are Black male faculty and serve as templates or models of how they can advance their academic careers while maintaining their self-respect, being their authentic selves, and—importantly to BMDS—maintain their authentic Blackness. This authenticity counters the passivity that socialization at times seems to subtly suggest. The Black male doctoral students in this study felt pressured to become less radical in their views, but is doctoral education seeking to create passive Black Ph.D.s or is the lesson more nuanced? For some, the takeaway messages have more to do with appropriately handling grievances and learning how to effectively navigate politically charged environments to achieve your desired goal.

Carrying the Mantle

Race remains a salient part of the identities and experiences of Black male doctoral students. Corey explained how race shapes his opportunities and how he intends to work to discover ways to continue to effectively close the academic achievement gap. He would love to do this as an academic, but he also refuses to put all of his "eggs in that basket":

> I had a professor say to me recently, "What do you want to do when you graduate; is it possible that you would want to go into academia?" I said, "Yeah that's definitely a possibility." He said, "Do you not know for sure?" I was like, "I'm not certain, but I want to have that door open." Then he stated, and I have had other people say this too, "Well if you want to go into academia, you need to focus on the academic route." I have had people tell me that I shouldn't work and I shouldn't get so involved in all of these organizations and focus on my academic work so I can be marketable when I finish. I have been socialized to believe the opposite.

Corey speaks of "being socialized to believe the opposite," however he is not referring to his academic socialization, but rather his socialization as a Black man. He expounds on that statement by underscoring the belief that as a Black man in a professional setting, he will often need to do more than others simply to be viewed as qualified and competent:

> I needed to do these things to make myself marketable. Going back to grade school, I have always believed that I needed to do the extra stuff and those were the things that got me a lot of attention. I always did well academically, but it wasn't until I was more outgoing and more social. You may hear this sometime where people say when referring to Black people, "He's so articulate" or "She's so well-spoken" and its usually not focused on your academic abilities as much but it's usually focused on your social abilities or how well you fit in with mainstream society. Sometimes I felt that the only way I was able to exhibit that was through my involvement in organizations.

Corey is arguing that the things he does beyond what is required of anyone is what sets him apart despite the fact that his academics alone or his publications alone should make him competitive. This echoes the African American community's long-held view that Blacks need to be twice as good to be considered as mere equals. Embedded in his argument is the notion that there is a deficit perspective that comes into play when he, as a Black male, is being evaluated in comparison with a White male. This deficit perspective is likely to include narratives about the Black male's intelligence, being a less collegial team member, and possibly being admitted because of Affirmative Action into his undergraduate institution and/or doctoral program. As a result of this deficit perspective, he feels that he needs additional work experience and credentials to bolster his academic record and combat these negative stereotypes.

For Black male doctoral students, carrying the mantle also means conducting research that is related to race, but doing it in a way that is beyond reproach in terms of quality. Earnest explains that he sees himself as following in the tradition of earlier Black scholars, which means that his work needs to be extremely well done because, at least in some ways, it represents the Black race:

> Talking to old-school Black Ph.D.s, I found that they are really serious about their work. They really believe that your work has to be tight because they grew up when it was really tough on them. They had to hold the mantle of the entire race and their work had to be really tight so that they can be legitimized. In that regard, everybody's pushing me and pushing me to be rigorous with my work. I know it has to be rigorous because my work hasn't been done by anyone else before.

For Earnest and other Black male doctoral students, race still matters. Black male doctoral students continue to feel that they must do more and present more rigorous work if they are to gain respect as academics, move their careers forward, and make a difference for Black communities and students.

CONCLUSION

The dominant perspective is that socialization is necessary and good for doctoral students if they are to move forward to have successful careers as faculty. While it is true that doctoral students need mentorship, training, and intellectual development, many of the social and cultural cues associated with socialization may be problematic for students of color. If Black doctoral students are to resist socialization and still find success, they will often need to find alternative routes of success, often with the assistance and mentorship of Black faculty.

A primary concern of critical race theory is the transformation of structural and cultural aspects of education (Solórzano & Yosso, 2002; Love, 2010). Similarly, a central concern for this study's participants has been navigating, resisting, and transforming many of the structural and cultural aspects of doctoral socialization that they as Black males find to be detrimental. BMDSs in this study have largely adopted proactive strategies to aid them in their academic careers. Most have sought strategic relationships with faculty, Black faculty in particular, as well as community support networks. Most have either created or worked closely with organizations that seek to transform the experiences of graduate students. These efforts are to maintain control of their educational experiences and resist elements of doctoral socialization that can be dehumanizing, frustrating, and isolating for students of color, while hopefully leaving the department and institution easier to navigate for those who follow in their footsteps.

REFERENCES

Benny, M., and E. C. Hughes (1970). Of sociology and the interview. In N.K. Denzin (ed.) *Sociological Methods: A Sourcebook* (pp. 175-181). Chicago: Aldine.

Bogdan, R.C., & Biklen, S.K. (2003). *Qualitative research for education: An introduction to theories and methods* (4th ed.). Boston: Pearson.

Bowen, W. G., Kurzweil, M. A., & Tobin, E. M. (2005). *Equity and excellence in American higher education.* Charlottesville and London: University of Virginia Press.

Bolman, L. G., and Deal, T. E. (2008). *Reframing organizations: Artistry, choice and leadership* (4th ed). San Francisco: Jossey-Bass.

Cashin, S. (2004). *The failures of integration: How race and class are undermining the American dream.* New York, NY: Public Affairs.

Creswell, J. W. (1998). *Qualitative inquiry and research design: Choosing among five traditions.* London, UK: Sage.

Creswell, J. W. (2007). *Qualitative inquiry & research design: Choosing among five approaches* (2nd ed.). Thousand Oaks, CA: Sage.

Cuyjet, M. J. (2006). *African American men in college.* San Francisco, CA: Jossey-Bass.

Denzin, N., & Lincoln, Y. (2000). Introduction: The discipline and practice of qualitative research. In N. Denzin & Y. Lincoln (Eds.), *Handbook of qualitative research* (2nd ed., pp. 1–28). Thousand Oaks, CA: Sage.

Feagin, J. R., & Sikes, M. P. (1995). How Black students cope with racism on white campuses. *The Journal of Blacks in Higher Education, 8*: 6.

Freire, P. (1970). *Pedagogy of the oppressed.* New York, NY: Continuum Publishing.

Gardner, S. K. (2007). "I heard it through the grapevine": Doctoral student socialization in chemistry and history. *Higher Education, 54,* 723–740.

Gardner, S. K. (2008). Fitting the mold of graduate school. *Innovative Higher Education, 33,* 125–138.

Golde, C. M. (1998). Beginning graduate school: Explaining first year doctoral attrition. In M. S. Anderson (Ed.), *The experience of being in graduate school: An exploration* (pp. 55–64). San Francisco, CA: Jossey-Bass.

Gonzalez, J. C. (2006). Academic socialization experiences of Latina doctoral students: A qualitative understanding of support systems that aid and challenges that hinder the process. *Journal of Hispanic Higher Education, 5*(4), 347–365.

Grutter v. Bollinger, 539 U.S. 306 (2003).

Harris, A. L. (2006). I (don't) hate school: Revisiting oppositional culture theory of Black resistance to schooling. *Social Forces, 85(2),* 797–834.

Harper, S. (2008). Realizing the intended outcomes of Brown: High-achieving African American male undergraduates and social capital. *American Behavioral Scientist, 51,* 1030–1053.

Hurtado, S. (1992). The campus racial climate: Context of conflict. *The Journal of Higher Education, 63*(5, Racial harassment on campus): 539-569.

Jencks, C., & Phillips, M. (1998). *The Black-White test score gap.* Washington: The Brookings Institution.

Journal of Blacks in Higher Education (2006). *Doctoral Degree Awards to African Americans Reach Another All-Time High.* Retrieved from http://www.jbhe.com/news_views/50_black_doctoral-degrees.html

Kaba, A. (2005). The gradual shift of wealth and power from African American males to African American females. *The Journal of African American Studies, 9*(3), 33–44.

Lincoln, Y., & Guba, E. (1986). But is it rigorous? Trustworthiness and authenticity in naturalistic evaluation. In D. Williams (Ed.), *Naturalistic evaluation* (pp. 73–84). San Francisco, CA: Jossey-Bass.

Love, B. J. (2004). Brown plus 50 counter-storytelling: A critical race theory analysis of the "majoritorian achievement gap" story. *Equity and Excellence in Education, 37,* 227-246.

Merton, R. K., Reader, G. G., and Kendall, P. L. (1957). *The student physician.* Cambridge, MA: Harvard University Press.

National Center for Education Statistics (2014). Table 324.20. Doctor's degrees conferred by postsecondary institutions, by race/ethnicity and sex of student: Selected years, 1976-77 through 2011-12. Retrieved on November 2, 2014, from http://nces.ed.gov/programs/digest/d13/tables/dt13_324.20.asp

Nettles, M. T., & Millett, C. M. (2006). *Three magic letters: Getting to Ph.D.* Baltimore, MD: The Johns Hopkins University Press.

Nettles, M. T. (1989). *Comparing the backgrounds, educational experiences and outcomes of Black, Hispanic and White doctoral students.* College Park, MD: National Center for Postsecondary Governance and Finance.

Patton, M. Q. (2002). *Qualitative research and evaluation methods* (3rd ed). Thousand Oaks, CA: Sage.

Perna, L. W. (2000). Differences in decisions to attend college among African Americans, Hispanics and Whites. *The Journal of Higher Education 71*(2, Special Issue: The Shape of Diversity): 117-141.

Porter, J. R. (2006). State flagship universities do poorly in enrolling and graduating Black men, report says. *Chronicle of Higher Education, 53*(8): 1.

Solórzano, D. G., & Yosso, T. J. (2002). Critical race methodology: Counter-storytelling as an analytical framework for education research. *Qualitative Inquiry, 8*, 23–44.

Stein, E. L. (1992). Socialization at a protestant seminary. Ph.D. dissertation, University of Pittsburgh.

Taylor, S. J., & Bogdan, R. (1998). *Introduction to qualitative research methods: A guidebook and resources* (3rd ed.). New York: John Wiley & Sons.

Thornton, R., & Nardi, P. M. (1975). The dynamics of role acquisition. *American Journal of Sociology. 80(4)*, 870-885.

Tierney, W. G. (1999, Winter). Models of minority college-going and retention: Cultural integrity versus cultural suicide. *The Journal of Negro Education 68*(1): 80–91.

Tinto, V. (1994). *Leaving college: Rethinking the causes and cures of student attrition* (2nd ed.). Chicago, IL: The University of Chicago Press.

Weidman, J. C. (1989). Undergraduate socialization: A conceptual approach. In J. C. Smart (Ed.), *Higher education: Handbook of theory and research* (Vol. 5, pp. 289–322). New York, NY: Agathon.

Weidman, J. C., Twale, D. J., & Stein, E. L. (2001). *Socialization of graduate students: A perilous passage?* San Francisco, CA: Jossey-Bass.

Weidman, J. C., & Stein, E. L. (2003). Socialization of doctoral students to academic norms. *Research in Higher Education, 44*(6), 641–656.

CHAPTER SEVEN

Pimp or Pauper: An Autoethnography of Black Gangstaism's Prevalence With College-Going Black Males at One Historically White Institution

STANLEY ELLIS

A LOWER LEARNING IN HIGHER EDUCATION

"Dude! I'm a Pimp!!" is the mantra that I chanted across my college's quad, with my Black male cohorts echoing my chant, mostly in unison. Each of us attempted to assert our dominance through the sheer volume of our statements. I spent six years at my predominantly White institution (PWI) engaging in this and similar manhood-professing behaviors. Little did I know that my friends and I were demanding our invitation into Black gangsta culture. Cureton (2009) described Black gangstaism as a social network institution where Black males participate in structured rites of passage that signify their transition from boyhood to manhood with the intent to mitigate the social oppression, isolation, resource strain, and denial of rights, freedoms, economic access, and social legitimacy they suffer because of their social class and skin color. Through my actions, I was immersing myself deeper into the Black gangstaism that had been so well crafted before my arrival at college in the mid-1990s and that I was so willing to perpetuate during my tenure at the institution even through graduation. The conviction evidenced through my behavior and my unwavering gangsta mindset was only one form my expression of manhood—the construction of manhood I had been socialized to believe.

I had seen this type of behavior be accepted and exhibited by men more senior than me and "cooler" than me. In this context, I use the term cool to mean those Black males who had earned the respect of other Black males on campus because of their toughness, wit, attitudes, and above all, their ability to date and have sex with multiple women. As a freshmen coming to college and seeing this, I wanted this status also, and eventually achieved it. Little did I know that my participation in the campus community's "gangsta" culture or gangstaism would leave me without either of my academic scholarships and an earned 1.38 first semester GPA. It was evident that as my status increased in the campus's gangsta culture, my academic achievements decreased. The two objects of my existence at the time had become inversely proportional.

According to Oliver (2006), "There are three masculine roles that constitute the core of the hierarchy of manhood roles that are valued by Black males who seek social recognition in the streets. These roles include the tough guy/gangsta, the player [pimp], and the hustler/balla" (p. 928). I used each of these roles to form my "cool pose." These roles are not mutually exclusive and, with little thought to my actions, I invoked the persona and behaviors of the role I needed to play to adapt to the situation I found myself in at any given moment. To be accepted by the cool-posing group of Black males on campus, I acted as they did. This meant I chose to behave tough and aggressively, focus on material wealth, and mask my emotions while engaging in constrained relationships with women (Harris, Palmer, & Struve, 2011). This meant that sometimes I was a gangsta, other times a balla, and most times, a pimp. I learned the art of cool posing and I practiced it well. I used my cool pose to graduate to pimp status in the campus's gangsta culture and I relished it. While I was pimping, my grades were plummeting.

My fall from grace coupled with the disappointment of my mother and closest brother lasted throughout the Christmas Holiday break. Their disappointment alone shocked me back to the young scholar that I had been prior to attending college. I never earned less than a 3.0 GPA for the rest of my academic life. I had become determined to regain my academic footing. I never missed a party, yet inconceivably, I achieved balance. I remember very vividly one occurrence where there was a party on a Thursday night and I had an exam first thing the following Friday morning. To ensure my success on the exam, I studied before the party. I returned to my dorm room inebriated close to 5am that Friday morning. I had enough faculties about myself to study more before the exam that would be taking place at 8am. I made it to the exam on time and passed the exam with a better-than-average grade. Now, I do not advocate for practicing this type of behavior to succeed academically. However, I do encourage one to employ the perseverance I demonstrated by studying through my self-inflicted inebriation and achieving a better-than-average grade on my exam.

CLASS ACTS

Harper (2004) described a sect of college-going Black males who had a history of academic achievements, leadership activities, and service to the Black community during their higher education experiences. He also described how the plight of this group was different from many Black males who were similar to me and my peers—the "gangstas." We were occupied with expressing our masculinities by "pursuing short-term sexual relationships with women, competing in male-dominated activities, and accumulating and displaying material possessions" (Harris, Palmer, & Struve, 2011, p. 48). I think it is important to note here that gangstaism was and still is a male-dominated culture that we engaged in 24 hours a day, seven days a week. Similar to how sports participation, club membership, and organizational affiliation are considered "the other curriculum" in higher education, gangstaism was included in my "other curriculum." For me and many of my Black male cohorts this was more than an elective. It was a second major.

Within my group of Black males, I quickly realized that my experiences were the only ones similar to those of the Black males Harper (2004) investigated. Although I likened my academic and leadership experiences with theirs, I cautioned myself against assuming that their socioeconomic status prior to entering college and the demographic composition of their communities of origin were the same as mine. I wondered if the only duality they experienced was the one described by W. E. B. Du Bois's idea of the double consciousness, or if these men endured the duality I experience. I wondered how similar or dissimilar our upbringings were and how their college experiences affected their identities. Finally, I wondered about their encounters with gangsta culture and their ability to navigate it without acquiescence. Either way, I applaud the strength of Harper's cohort of Black college males. Obviously, I was unaware of my ability to harness the mental fortitude that Harper's cohorts possessed; or, if I am going to be honest, the truth is that the gangsta culture was alluring and I allowed it to seduce away my logic and better judgment with regard to establishing my masculinity.

Harris, Palmer, and Struve (2011) sought to discover how Black males on college campuses who do not assume leadership roles and were not student-athletes expressed their masculinities. Unfortunately for me, I made the mistake of attempting to validate my masculinity in both the academic and leadership arena, while excelling in the gangstaism of the campus, by subscribing to the criteria of both personas. I was a member of several campus organizations, including my fraternity. I organized community service activities to serve the Black population within the city. While I was initiating and engaging in these admirable leadership activities, I was ever searching for another opportunity—another female conquest—to foster my identity as a part of the "gangsta" sect. My primary expression of masculinity was through my transient, sexual relationships with women, both on and off campus. For me, my leadership and academics created opportunities to meet and seduce more women, continuing to elevate my pimp status—my eliteness. My membership in the elite Black Greek fraternity on campus only bolstered my status. The culmination of the power I had acquired—through my academic achievements, relationships with school administrators, social capital, and my fraternal leadership—was all amazingly seductive. The more I drank from the cup of power that came with having high status in the campus's gangsta culture, the more I enjoyed it and the deeper I willingly sank into its quickening sands.

A GANGSTA TRAGEDY

Following a discussion of my intentions to write this autoethnography and the subject of its content, a colleague of mine was inspired to describe his own seduction by the same Black gangsta pimp culture I had participated in and which I had a hand in crafting for him and his cohorts as their predecessor on the same college campus. He illuminates here the familiar attraction that I and many other Black males found with Black Greek life—and its possible pitfalls:

My reason for questing to college was "knot" the searching for knowledge
From the days prior to taking the ACT., after receiving the results, not even after signing through admissions and registering for my first fourteen credits, not on the day did myself and numerous others stood circling these tall brick buildings with a white map in our hand that read only two letters three numbers, did any professor be the first to greet me
Neither I nor the others were ready for war
We were the uneducated soldiers waiting for a commander, waiting for a leader
Not knowing we were our own leaders
So I stood looking and listening to my reason for standing on the campus
The marching band came through from different units, all playing separate but similar tunes
16 boots sounded from the pounding off the ground of gladiators screaming in a language spoken many years ago "Que Psi Phiiiiii"
22 other soldiers rushed the zone; their color coordination, precision to each movement of the legs and the arms
They began calling us in "This is where you wanna be, Blue Phi, Blue Phi"
Quietly these gentlemen of aristocracy glided across the cement path to class blocking my vision of doors destination that I was supposed to enter
They let white and red canes dangle from their arms

The one raised his cane to his chest forming some sort of sign with his hand yelling "Yo sweet Nupe" while a brother beside him began gracefully wielding two canes as swords
That's not where it ended
The descendants of Imhotep stood behind me, they dressed as the elite, Black and adorned with gold
Each of their eyes seem to be laying upon me
"1–1–1–1–9… 0–6, 0–6" they spoke
I was ready to part the audience and climb the stairs to the class door
Then Sirens exited the glass door
One passed, then two more, then came 4, and more
Three women's units, they sang to me
Laced with Ivy, pink and green "what does skeeee-weeee" mean
Just let them sing
A.K.A.s they were
Let the beauty of these determined, destined, bold women placing their hands in diamond shape as if that's what they were worth… and yes, I would have bought diamonds for each of them,
Deltas they were
I watched doves fly from above with blue ribbons on their wings
Lord the Sirens sing sweet music to my ears
Zeta what, Zeta who, Zeta them
I should have parted the campus hours ago
I had missed three classes and that wasn't to be the last time

The freshmen Greek show, freshmen street dance
The women were fresh meat, Damn!
Girls with their hands on their knees asses popping up and down, heads rolling
I don't know the two in front of me but they look as if they are ready to make their way to the bedroom
Some guy said to me "Damn, they on you playa"…
Playa… yep, I was about to become that… a Playa
A party every night
Along with the occasional fight
Leaving the Financial Aid office with a large check in my hand
I asked two women out
I was the f'in' man
I called two other "broads" ready to get down for the night
There was another party we were headed to, a Pajama Jammy Jam
I was about to be on… and I was
I was on two A.K.A.s, one Zeta, two Deltas, and there were four others I spotted but didn't get their names or numbers because I had too much liquor in the SOLO cup
Yep, you guessed it
Tomorrow came or at least I thought it was tomorrow
I had missed class for the past two weeks
I hadn't been to choir practice from singing my own tune of praise and glory
Drop notices came by email
"What the hell?"
My GPA went straight down the toilet with one quick flush

"This aint funny"
I was mesmerized by the money,
Loved by the honeys
Envied by the fellas that couldn't seem to catch up on the trail I was on
They just didn't know what trail I was on
With my grades in the crapper
No matter how dapper I looked
College to me… was nowhere close to a book
Yep, listening to the songs of the Sirens, I crashed into the rocks
Watching the Greeks pull off stepping stunts, had my mind blocked
So with a couple more cups of this Incredible Hulk, I didn't give a…
Forget some class
Forget some grades
Forget a major and a minor
I had been tied up in a "Knot", didn't know that I was sure to hang myself
I was truly a Playa' who had played himself
It was a new fall semester, four years after my admission and registration
Most of my peers were buying caps and gowns for spring graduation
I was still a sophomore
I looked at the campus and saw the same Play start all over again
Different actors, same parts
So I headed to class, Advanced Western Literature
The topic was Homer and Shakespeare
The "Gods" and the "Tragedies"
I guess this is college. (R. Davis-Buckley, personal communication, November 8, 2013)

This depiction of college life, expression of Black masculinity and Black gangstaism culture on our historically White campus, is more accurate than some may desire to believe or remember; however, for me, this depiction is more precise than not. The fraternity was a pedestal made of egos, admirers, brotherhood, sexual allure, and popularity. It allowed us to create "god-like" personas among our peers that were rarely contested. This depiction of fraternities is not at all to minimize the actual purpose of the establishment. It is simply to express the responsibility that came with the letters we strapped across our chest that I and my brothers should have taken more seriously.

Young Black freshmen males who stood atop our hallowed grounds were inundated with the sea of vibrant colors that we donned to signify our elite status as Black Greeks. Our Black Greek affiliations provided us, as Black males, a vehicle through which we perpetuated our gangsta culture and facilitated our recruitment processes. Greek organizations were infrastructures for gangsta socialization more than they were for civic leadership, academic achievement, or community service. Part of the gangstaism narrative, which was fed to our unsuspecting pledges, was the belief that in order to date Black female Greeks, they would have to be members of a Black male Greek organization. The culture portrayed these ideal

Black Greek males as strong, successful, and sexually attractive, while the ideal Black females were defined as simply physically attractive sexual objects (Hazell & Clarke, 2008). As the poem above vividly illustrates, gangster culture was made much more alluring with the addition of the Black Greek "sirens," who sang their sweet songs that drew the outsiders closer to what they longed for—what we all had longed for—to be accepted as men.

    I enjoyed my social eliteness so much that I graduated twice from college to prolong the inevitable—leaving. I acquired my bachelor's degree with a double major in four years. I attended summer school every year to achieve this feat. I refused to be a statistic. My first semester failure and the disappointed silence I suffered from my family members left me with nothing less than sheer determination. I even attended an intense, two-week course during a pre-summer session so that I could graduate on time. However, I had ulterior motives for attending that session. I wanted to reap the benefits of my top position in our gangsta culture. I wanted to use my time in summer school, including the two-week session, to add to my long list of female conquests—the most revered benefit of my rank. It was my intent to soak up as much of the benefits of being a general in the campus's gangsta culture as I possibly could. My status and the gratification that came with it made me quickly realize, as I approached my undergraduate graduation, that I was about to have to leave all of the benefits of my position behind. I was not ready to do that yet, so I decided to stay at the institution and get a master's degree. This would provide me two more years on the campus in my position as a top dog (no fraternal affiliation intended)—a major "pimp." Thus, I continued my gangsta exploits another two years—including summers.

    Of course, simply living in the city where I went to school would have afforded me the ability to be on the campus when I wanted, but without the legitimacy of being a student. I was smart and I was on a successful trajectory academically and professionally. I recognized early on that my intellectual allure bolstered my gangsta persona. This was evident to those around me, especially to my female companions. To stay near the college or around the college without being a student would have denigrated my status and denied me full participation in the Black gangsta culture that my peers and I had so perfectly appended to our very un-unique collegiate experiences. Besides, I had seen what happened to an older gangsta who came to campus without actually being enrolled in school. He simply looked old, desperate, and unaware of his irrelevance. Being old is not a negative characteristic of a gangsta; however, being desperate is pathetic. To be both was the death knell to his gangsta status. This combination of age and desperation stripped this gangsta of his pimp card. I witnessed his constant struggle to regain his status to no avail. Even when he thought he had it, he did not. He was constantly ridiculed and mocked by females and his peers, myself included. Without the primary defensive weapon of the gangsta culture at his disposal, he was unable to defend himself. He had no harem. He had no entourage. He was no longer a gangsta.

Now this gangsta culture may seem trivial and somewhat of a caricature of real college life; however, I assure you that this culture on my college campus, and I suspect other college campuses as well, was very real. The preceding paragraphs only provide a pinhole view into the importance of Black gangstaism in the life of Black males on predominantly White college campuses. However, my introduction to Black gangstaism and its sub-culture of pimpin' began way before I ever stepped one foot on a college campus. I am convinced that most other Black males received their introduction to this same culture prior to entering college. In essence, my story is not very different from the stories of other young Black males who experience similar upbringings. In other respects, my story is different. I aim to share how this culture shaped my upbringing as a young Black boy and my existence as a young Black adult male. As I describe my life's journey from childhood to adulthood, I hope to illustrate the importance of my academic achievements to my story and how Black gangsta culture influenced many facets of my journey and the journeys of my Black male peers.

EMERGENCE OF DUALITY

I remember a time during my youth, from kindergarten to about sixth grade, when school was virtually easy to me. It was fun. I found my assignments to be less than challenging—most of the time. I always finished early and oftentimes with a perfect score on the assignment. This allowed me the time to be mischievous while other students struggled with their work. Sometimes, my mischief would disrupt the progress of my fellow classmates. This seemed to be a common occurrence in my classes. Although I got in trouble for my disruptive behaviors, I was rarely sanctioned severely, simply because of my well-mannered demeanor and my academic accomplishments. I learned at an early age that I could skirt most reprimands with my charming ways while relying on my intellectual merit as my saving grace.

Cozart (2010) described how she compartmentalized her personal and professional life as a means of reconciling her spirituality. I used Cozart's perspective of compartmentalization as a means to keep separate my academic and public persona from my street or gang behaviors. I was also attempting to balance my internal dissonance and avoid choosing one persona over the other. I was already adept in the academic and intellectual pursuits needed for the survival of my public persona. It was the street culture that I needed to become more familiar and comfortable with. Therefore, I immersed myself deeper into the gangsta culture of my neighborhood community. I never planned to stray too far from my safe and socially acceptable behaviors into the gangstaism street lifestyle. I created for myself a tunnel between both worlds where I could operate on both sides as freely as I liked, as a sort of double agent if you will, with the sole intent of serving myself. In short, I was "code switching." I was being who and what I needed to be in the public eye and being who and what I needed to be in the streets. I was fooling myself to believe that I could dabble in street life—in promiscuity, alcohol, and other immoral activities—and then return to my successful academic endeavors without repercussions. All the while, I was trying to convince myself that what I was doing was okay and necessary for my survival. In actuality, my "code switching" was leading to my social, emotional, and spiritual deterioration.

Although I often engaged in mischievous activities, I had the foresight to know how close to get to the line without crossing it. Most of my peers did not. I learned early that it was important for me to build positive relationships with my teachers and the administrators of my schools. There were times when my superintendent of schools trusted me to the point that she would allow me to run errands for the school in her brand new Dodge truck. I found that to be an honor—and an ego inflator as well. It was not until around the 10th or 11th grade that I really saw how different I was from my classmates. I was in social studies class and my high school principal walked in, scanned the room, and he noticed that several other students and I were off task and talking. He looked in our direction and stated, "While y'all are over there smoking and joking with Ellis, Ellis is going to get his work done and you will still be trying to get finished" (H. Mayo, personal communication, 1993). I encountered my high school principal in my hometown while in the midst of writing this chapter. I reminded him of that incident, the statement he made, and the impact it had on me. He remembered the statement vividly and reiterated, "That's right. They were going to still be trying to get their lesson done after you had finished" (H. Mayo, personal communication, November 2, 2013). I informed him that during that particular incident, I had already completed my assignment. This was the first time that I realized that I was different in many respects from my peers. This early revelation followed me throughout my academic career. Unbeknownst to me, the dichotomy I created and cherished and my existence in two worlds would hinder my educational, professional, and spiritual growth.

It subconsciously became my mission to disprove the myth that it was not cool to be smart. It seemed trivial that one had to choose between being one or the other. This was before I even knew that such a myth existed. I knew it was cool to be smart. As a youth in school, I engaged in aberrant behaviors with my friends. We were essentially a gang, regardless of how much I tried to discount our actual makeup. We were a gang in a very small town with a population of less than 800 people. Our primary focus was to get girls and, in the event you were someone whom we did not like, rival gang or any individual, we would "gank" you or steal your belongings—thus the creation of our name Gank Mob. If you were a foe, you may have found some of your items missing without a trace, all the while we were in your company and you were oblivious to the fact you had been ganked. There were six of us in total. Unlike my friends, if we were ever caught, I could fall back on my academics and stellar community and school reputation to help lessen or exonerate me from any punitive actions that would be imposed. Better yet, I was the most unlikely to be suspected of such actions. I enjoyed my status even as an adolescent. I was the smartest of our gang academically; however, each of my cohorts was more adept at maneuvering the street culture than I.

During my junior high and high school years, we would ride around our four-street town in my cousin's 1988 Oldsmobile, pumping out the sounds from the lyrics of the Geto Boys "Straight Gangstaism" that were for the most part indicative of our existence:

> I used to hang out by the ballroom and study the gangsta style …
> I let 'em influence me, and my momma hated it,
> (Geto Boys, 1993, Track 10)

I look back now and I see how pervasive Black gangstaism was in my life. I realize now how the music my friends and I listened to influenced our behaviors, personas, and our cool pose. We often tried to be the gangstas in the rap music we listened to. But for me, I was simply posing. My friends on the other hand, they maintained these personas without fail or falter. It was to my detriment to return to my mother's house with any street behaviors still flowing in my veins. The only times I saw my friends dispense with their street personas were when they came to my house and were in the presence of my mother. I guess they knew how to code switch, too.

ROLE MODELS AND ROLLING STONES

It was not until later in my life that I found out I had 20 sisters and brothers. My mother had seven children and I was the youngest. There is a 13-year age difference between me and my closest brother, on my mother's side of the family. It was not until I was 13-years-old that my mother told me about my father and my other siblings. How typical of impoverished, small town, Black community behavior that my father and his family, including his wife, my brothers, sisters, nieces, and nephews all lived three houses down from me on the same street. I had been playing with my relatives all this time and even liking one of my nieces. Once I found out about my other family, I also found out that I had a brother who was closer to me in age. He and I shared the exact same birthday and we were exactly nine years apart, with him being older. None of these revelations angered me in the least. In fact, they had the opposite effect. I had more family that I could enjoy, was my thought. Now the realization did hit me that I had never considered any of my brothers or sisters born to my mother half-siblings. I felt the same way about my siblings born to my father. If you were my brother or sister, you were my brother or sister. Period. However, the brothers and sisters born to my father were 14 in number and all of those were not by his wife.

So as you can see, from an early age, I learned infidelity was commonplace in male-female relationships. Maybe, my father's sexual behaviors can be explained through Wallace's (2007) theory that Black men's need and "ability to engage in patriarchal sex that emphasizes conquest, and the ability to spread their seed to make babies serves to remedy the lack of control and power Black men have in larger society and functions as an arena in which they can seek fulfillment, power and affirmation" (p. 17). I learned the pimping game from my father and my brothers. I learned in the early 1980s what Collins (2004) declared a common lesson in Black culture for young Black boys, which was that I should have as much sex as possible with as many women as possible as acts of professing my manhood. Although I did not know that my father was my father at the time, I knew him and he was one of the "pimps" in the community who I observed regularly. Essentially, my father was a ghetto superstar of my community and whether he or my brothers knew it, their actions influenced the man I grew to be—sexual, promiscuous, aggressive. A pimp. A gangsta.

Cureton (2009) believed that "Black Americans who exist outside of the American Dream have historically had a direct relationship with street revolutionaries and ghetto superstars more than the appointed Black leadership" (p. 347). I find this to be particularly true because the "American Dream" was far from the reach of the Black families in my small town. This dream was not something that the majority of the adults in my community sought to achieve. Their complacency filtered down to their children as well and thus, the "American Dream" was only a myth for many of us. To this day, I can name 90% of the ghetto superstars, the pimps, and gangstas of my community. I cannot name even one male figure that was considered positive Black leadership in our community.

My father was one of our neighborhood ghetto superstars because of the number of women he had. My uncles, my father's brothers, shared this path of female exploitation and fathering children out of wedlock, including me. Closer to me emotionally and physically than my father and uncles were my four maternal brothers, two of whom were ghetto superstars in my community because of their toughness and their exploits with women. One brother (one of my mother's sons) in particular received the same ghetto superstar status as my father, maybe even surpassed him. My brothers, my father, and my uncles were the people I related and looked up to. I internalized their personas and behaviors—towards women and life—to some degree, more with my female exploits, but less with my outlook on life. They were my conduits of male gender role socialization. They were my examples and I was anxious to be like them and, soon enough, I would have my chance.

I remember every Fourth of July holiday because it seemed like Christmas. All of my brothers would come home. Being the youngest, this always excited me. This was my chance to hang out with my brothers. Every time they would come home, each of them would bring their gun in the house and hand it over to our mother for safe keeping, primarily for the safe keeping of anyone who may challenge them during this festive time. All of them would do this except for one. He never really cared for guns much, and it is ironic given his current profession of law enforcement. I could not wait until the day that I came home on the Fourth of July holiday and handed over my gun to my mother. This was to me affirmation that I was now able to roll with my big brothers. I considered them tough and I wanted to be like them.

I grew up hearing stories of how one of my brothers went to jail every other weekend, on schedule and without fail, for attempting to shoot one of his adversaries. I was told stories of another of my brothers having a habit of shooting at the enemies of his brothers. I had been told stories of another brother who was considered the "silent but deadly" one. He was quiet, but he knew martial arts and was pretty good with nunchucks. I witnessed firsthand the manhood of my closest maternal brother as he exerted his toughness and dominance over some guy at a football game one night in his attempt to protect me, his little brother. The guy kept kicking me while my brother and I attempted to enjoy the football game. I alerted my brother that I was being kicked and he immediately threatened to fight the guy. Needless to say, the kicks stopped immediately. I was proud of my brother and thankful. I contacted him recently as I thought about including this story in this chapter. His male bravado response was, "Are you going through something?" (D. Williams, personal communication, November 20, 2013). I was showing my appreciation for his defense of his little brother; however, his male toughness prevented him from simply saying thank you.

I also remember an incident where we were all home again on the Fourth of July. This particular year, I had obtained a .380 caliber pistol while I was at college which was not registered. I could not wait to come home and relinquish it to my mother like I had seen the rest of my brothers do so many times before. I was really one of them now. Unfortunately, this was a year where some local thug attacked one of my brothers because my brother had physically bested him at the club the night before. This was the thug's payback. My brothers had gone to the liquor store and I happened to be at home with my mother. Very abruptly, they returned to the house and two of them hopped out of the car and ran inside. I knew immediately that this could only mean one thing—there was about to be trouble. They had come for their arsenal. They returned outside as abruptly as they went in. After seeing this, I ran in the house to get my gun as well. As I returned outside, my brother who had been attacked talked to me in an attempt to calm me down. As I listened through the tears that rolled down my face, all I could think was that someone had hurt my brother, who had taken care of me as a kid, and who taught me how to tell time. I was hurt and I wanted to hurt whoever had hurt him. As they drove off, I stayed—until they got out of sight. My mother came outside with her pistol as well, and she and I both went looking for the culprit. We didn't find him. He hid so effectively in our little four-street town and you could tell that everyone who saw us knew our intentions.

"BE BETTER THAN ME"

I did not realize it then, but I realized it later in my life that my brothers were trying to protect me. They were trying to shield me from the "street" lifestyle they were actively engaging in at the time and the retaliation that would come with it. It was their hope that I would be better than the street life. They charged themselves with making sure that I had the chance to achieve that goal that seemed unobtainable. They wanted to ensure my success in college and in life. But, at that moment, all I wanted was to be a brother and for me, that chance was taken away. One of my brothers was absent from the Fourth of July festivities during this particular year. He made sure to come home the following week in hopes of finding the thug who attacked our brother. I met him in our hometown and we spent most of our time searching for the thug. Once again he evaded us, to his benefit. My street life has been more than most would imagine or believe.

Oliver (2006) described "the streets as an alternative site of Black male socialization...a formal and informal interactive process in which the adults in a society...deliberately seek to inculcate its young people with the beliefs, values, and norms that will allow them to functionally adapt as members of society" (p. 918). I adapted well. I adapted by drinking alcohol at an early age with my brothers and my mother. I always saw my mother, father, brothers, uncles, and neighbors drinking alcohol, some to the point of abusing it. It was our community's recreation—as it was and continues to be for many impoverished, low income Black communities in America. For communities like mine high rates of unemployment, underemployment, poverty, substance abuse, incarceration, dysfunctional families, and absent or inadequate father are largely indicative of lives lived in the streets for young Black males (Oliver, 2006). I can validate this because I do not remember my mother ever being employed in a job that provided a W-2. Yet, she always seemed to provide for her children. She would spend 8 to 10 hours a day in the cotton fields for $20 a day, $25 depending on the affluence of the White crop owner. My father figure growing up was my brother, who was 13 years my senior. Once I turned five years of age, he graduated and left for college, so for the next 13 years of my life, what I learned about being a man, came from my mother.

My mother was strict, therefore, for those next 13 years; the streets were not my home. Although I dabbled in street life, my home life was very stable, even without a father. The only thing I ever wanted for was a motorized scooter, which was obviously not a necessity. My mother never got me one. However, when I turned 17 in the 11th grade, she did buy me a new car instead. I never wanted for anything and very seldom (and I do mean very seldom) was I ever hungry. When I was hungry and food had become scarce, it only helped me to develop an appreciation for Delta syrup sandwiches and grilled cheese sandwiches with grape jelly spread, which I would fix for my friends sometimes when they were over at my house and hungry.

PIMP IN TRAINING

When I was five years old, we lived next door to a juke joint. There was only a common wall that separated our house and this social establishment. On the porch of my house there was a screen that I could peer through into the juke joint and see all the happenings that were taking place. My mother would frequent this place and others like it. I would often accompany her, like so many other kids did with their mothers. Many times, this is where we would get to see our fathers, our real fathers, who had real families in other houses within the city.

On the corner of the street perpendicular to ours was the pool hall and two more juke joints that lined the street alongside it. I greatly admired the man who ran the pool hall and he favored me as well. At the age of five, I decided to venture over and visit with him. There was only a very large hill with a steep decline that separated me from getting to him at the pool hall. I braved that feat one day without alerting my mother to my actions. Needless to say, when her five-year-old was nowhere in sight, she became quite alarmed. When I became an adult, my mother told me how she had questioned all the drunkards who hung in the alley, who would have seen me, including my father. They laughed at her without giving up my location. She did however, finally find me and I received the thrashing of a lifetime that lasted from the pool hall, across the street, and up the hill. The hill was much easier to get down than it was to get back up. Each time I slid down, my thrashing continued. I never tried that again. I wish my father had saved me from that beating, but I think he feared receiving a beating himself. My mother was one tough lady.

I had an older brother who was born to my mother that introduced me to the pimping game early in my life. I remember specifically one cold winter afternoon, the ground covered in snow, my brother took me outside on our screened porch and said to me, "stay here and come get me if you see a pretty woman come down the street" (L. Williams, personal communication, November 1982). This was my older brother and, as cold as it was to me at age seven, I did exactly as he asked. This single act was the beginning for me, the moment I started to act like the pimps, gangstas, and ghetto superstars in my community. I was suddenly aware of the gangsta culture around me and, like a sponge, I soaked it in. Reluctantly, I'll admit that this act showed me the extreme that a pimp sometimes needs to go to to conquer his female prey.

I acknowledge that I was in the midst of the Black gangsta pimp culture, physically and metaphorically. My community was composed of a majority of low- and working-class Black residents, as well as individuals who received welfare benefits. Of course, there were some White members of our small town, yet they were part of their own community on the other side of town. "Across the tracks" is what it is considered in most towns like mine. In this situation, surrounded by jukes and gangstas, I was inundated with gangsta pimp behaviors inside and outside of my home. Pleck and Pleck (1980) concluded that in Black communities similar to mine, working-class Black men place a great emphasis on their sexual promiscuities and sexual conquests. These behaviors were ritualized in a sense and served as a sort of orientation or rite of passage into the pimp circle, into a level of manhood that a Black male would not achieve in such a community without numerous sexual conquests (Majors & Mancini-Billson, 1992).

Gangsta pimp behaviors exhibited by the men in my life contributed to my belief that manliness was measured by how much sex you had and how many women you'd been with. Wallace (2007) contended that in communities such as mine, "sexuality for young boys helps to draw the inference for both boys and girls that manhood and masculinity are inherently sexual matters that for one to fully become a man, one need only engage in sexual intercourse" (p. 16). Looking back, I can see that this is likely the reason that I and many of my adolescent cohorts focused so much of our energy into trying to have sex for the first time and probably even more energy into lying about it and maintaining that lie. We wanted to be counted as men by the measuring stick that had been used as an example for us—a male's first sexual encounter with a woman.

PAUPERS IN PIMPS' CLOTHING

When I was asked to contribute my story to this volume, I was immediately transported to a time in college when nearly every Black male I knew, including myself, considered himself to be a pimp—measured by the number of female sexual partners he had had or because of the art of pimping that he practiced to acquire female partners. I began to consider how paradoxical it was that we claimed to be pimps. Here we were, in college, jobless and virtually penniless. Most of us were unemployed and relied heavily on assistance from our parents, mostly single mothers, or our student loan checks, which we only received at the beginning of each semester—and, which we spent by the second day of the same semester.

The college I attended was geographically located in a "dry county." Now, having been raised in a low socioeconomic, predominantly Black community where liquor was sold every day of the week either legally or illegally, I had no concept of what a "dry county" was. The first time I heard the phrase, I literally thought that it meant that the city did not get much rain. I quickly realized my ignorance. Since the city was in a "dry county," it was not uncommon for me and my friends to receive our student loan checks at the beginning of the semester, cash them, and travel to a liquor store in the neighboring city to spend upwards of $200 on liquor to support our habit. I personally prided myself on getting my loan check, cashing it, and being back on campus and ready to party by 9 a.m. the day checks were issued. However, for the most part, our habit was not drinking so much as it was the need to look like big shots, to look like we had money to blow—to look like gangstas.

As I initially reflected on this "I'ma pimp" chant that many of us screamed as we traversed our college campus, I thought it to be in contradiction to our actual financial situation. Financially, I was different. Even though I came to college from a low socioeconomic, single-parent home, I was not broke. I had joined the military as a junior in high school at the age of 17. To be honest, I had every military recruiting agency calling my house and I turned all of them down except the National Guard. Coming from a single parent home and knowing my mother could not afford to send me to college, even with the scholarships I received, the National Guard said the magic words that got me to enlist: "We'll give you money for college." I received both the G.I. Bill and my drill check each month during my four-year undergraduate program. In addition to this income, I had secured and maintained a work-study job on campus. To increase my income, I took a job in the cafeteria because it paid more than my work-study position did. At one point, I worked at a fast food restaurant that served taco burgers. In essence, I had three checks coming in each month. I have always maintained multiple streams of income, even now. However, my friends who claimed to be pimps generally suffered from financial distress.

Most of my peers, who attempted to actually employ the true art of pimping, by using their female conquests to support them, weren't able to secure much more than a water bill, partial light bill payment, or the occasional fast food meal. A friend of mine who attended college with me reinforced this reality during a conversation we had recently. He recalled:

> I was living with these two guys and their girls both had money, one because of the amount of scholarships she had and her father's professional position and the other because of an inheritance. The girls would come over and clean up and cook. These dudes thought that they were really pimpin' these girls because of this, but they couldn't get those girls to pay any bills. Finally, I had to tell them that those girls were coming over and cooking because they were hungry and they couldn't cook in the dorm where they lived, not because they were trying to feed them. I, on the other hand, had to show them how this pimpin' was done. I had my girl bring me and them food and pay my part of the bills. And they asked me how'd I get my girl to do that. Them cats weren't no pimps. I was a pimp. (A. Price, personal communication, October 16, 2013).

Gangstas and pimps use, or rather misuse women to support them financially. More often than not, though, my Black male friends were financially destitute. I either didn't recognize it at the time or I suppressed the knowledge that my peers were pseudo-gangstas, who used their female sex partners for sex, but more pointedly, as a display of their dominance among their male counterparts. Dominance was determined solely on the size of their harem. Based on the true definition of gangsta and pimp, I was no more of one than were my peers. I was also a pseudo-gangsta. Not one of us was supported financially by his female conquests. In some respect, my conviction that I was a gangsta would have dissipated had I realized that my peers were not gangstas. And so I avoided the truth. We were simply pseudo-gangstas, if that, and yet the fallacy of our "gangstaism" lived on.

I think, unconsciously, I learned early on in my college years that in the "streets"—or in the street culture we were perpetuating within our university—that being different or being in a better position than my peers, financially or academically, would mark me as a target for ridicule and a candidate for being ostracized. I would have been gradually pushed to the outside of the inner circles. Thinking on it now, this was true even as early as elementary school. So I did my best to keep my income and financial status a secret, simply to remain within the circle. However, I realized only a few years ago, as an adult, that I had been the subject of such ridicule for these very reasons by my fellow gangstas, despite my best efforts to avoid it. My success had exceeded theirs. My ostracism from the group and my personal success were inextricably linked.

I adopted and internalized the "I'ma pimp" mantra to fit in with my male contemporaries. Yet, I really thought myself to be different in the respect that I did not depend on my female sex partners to support me financially or otherwise. I was in this gangsta culture for the social status, bragging rights, and the sheer pleasure that came with the promiscuity. It was only later in my life, post-college, that I realized I was different in more than just this particular regard. However, this gangstaism proved to be so prevalent on my campus and in my life that I felt as if I had to play the role to be accepted and to be recognized as a major player. The benefits of being accepted as a gangsta may have seemed miniscule and trivial to those outside of our culture. They were definitely considered imperative to those of us who were on the inside and even more compelling to those seeking entry. The benefits operated as a sort of cultural collateral. The more I pimped, the more I added to my harem. The more females I had as sex partners, the more collateral I built in the streets. The cultural collateral included: (1) reverence among male peers and females for having many women; (2) earned respect of other males, those in my circle and those who were not; (3) defense against ridicule from peers because my sexual prowess evidenced my exceptional manhood, especially against peers who lacked such prowess; (4) increased likeliness of other females to be attracted to me because of my pimp reputation (ironic, yet true).

For me, the cultural collateral I earned meant that I was revered as a man among my peers. In addition to this, I was man to be envied. I had achieved the goal that each of us Black males had sought to obtain and to maintain. I had gained respect. I was immune to ridicule (at least to my face). I was less likely to be challenged either physically or verbally by my peers or those outside of my circle. I had proven myself and my reputation had permeated outside my immediate social circle. The reputation of my carnal prowess facilitated my ability to add to my female conquests. My goal of being a man—being the man—had been achieved.

ELLIS VS. DU BOIS

W. E. B. Du Bois (1903/1995) discussed the duality or double consciousness of being Black in a White world. Du Bois stated:

> ...the Negro is a sort of seventh son, born with a veil, and gifted with second-sight in this American world, a world which yields him no true self-consciousness, but only lets him see himself through the revelation of the other world. It is a peculiar sensation, this double-consciousness, this sense of always looking at one's self through the eyes of others, of measuring one's soul by the tape of a world that looks on in amused contempt and pity. One ever feels his twoness,—American, a Negro; two souls, two thoughts, two unreconciled strivings; two warring ideals in one dark body, whose dogged strength alone keeps it from being torn asunder... The history of the American Negro is the history of this strife,—this longing to attain self-conscious manhood, to merge his double self into a better truer self. (p. 45)

The duality that Du Bois describes was one that I did not readily understand; I could only see my own double consciousness as a Black male who dared desire to be great. My duality was rooted in my need to achieve academically, and yet be accepted socially by my peers. For me, the pressures of this particular dual consciousness greatly outweighed the duality described by Du Bois. As a young Black man in a predominantly Black, impoverished community in the rural South, Du Bois's double consciousness was far removed from me. What I experienced as a youth was immediate, active, and pervasive. The dogged strength, however, of this two-ness, my *two-ness*, is what kept me from falling victim to the perils of my impoverished community and the system that perpetuated the cycle of poverty and failure. Now, as an adult, I find myself in the midst of Du Bois's two-ness, and yet, only recently removed from my own. During my life, I warred with both my own duality that I had learned to maneuver since childhood, and the two-ness Du Bois illuminated more than a century ago. Certain spiritual and professional experiences forced me to only fight one battle—the one that would bring me and my family great reward. Removing myself from the struggle of my own dual consciousness was a choice that proved to be as difficult, if not more difficult than overcoming the dual consciousness by Du Bois. Although my first experience with this philosophy was self-imposed, it has been much harder to move forward from it than it has to exist in this life and country as a Black man, especially a Black man with a purpose for success.

Because of my academic achievements and my well-mannered public persona, White people, school, and public officials in my hometown and college community held me in high regard as a young man and as a student. My friends knew this and as a result, they would leverage my relationships with authority figures to help us in various situations where they themselves did not have the skills to maneuver the professional landscape. Throughout my academic career, my peers relied on me for academic support. When my fraternity was in trouble or when we needed to get something done with the institution's blessing, I was the "brother" that was commissioned for the task. I am sure that this is also the reason I was—at one point during my undergraduate education—elected president of my fraternity. I relished my position. I was "a man." I was *the man*. This gangstaism was a drug and just like any other drug, it became all-consuming and my spiritual fabric languished. Once I recognized the duality of my existence, I realized that this was a common plight among Black men. I also remembered from my church attendance as a young boy that no man can serve two masters. Therefore, I had to love one and hate the other.

Although, I graduated with two degrees in six years, I still could have focused more and established myself more professionally had I not exerted so much energy in living a dual existence. I think I entered college with the notion that I could work and play and still be successful. What the principal had said all those years ago had become a part of my identity—I could do both, be both, have it all. I obviously misinterpreted his words, or rather, I heard what satisfied my passions and validated the gangsta lifestyle that had community had been born into.

While we were pimps through our own convictions and the illusion we had created through our behavior, we were actually paupers; we were victims of the Black gangstaism we had been socialized in. We were also masters of perpetuating this culture on our campus and continuing the victimization of other unsuspecting young Black males who entered our quad, our hallowed halls of pimping that we created with the prior knowledge and experience that many of us acquired from the men in our communities: uncles, brothers, estranged fathers, unfaithful fathers. Even our mothers played a part in our indoctrination. We were then, as many of us continue to be now, leaders of the degradation and genocide of our young Black men, of our Black race as a whole.

RECOMMENDATIONS

Colleges and Universities. The Black gangsta culture on my predominantly White college campus was problematic for me and many of my young Black male cohorts. The more we engaged in the gangstaism of our White college campus community, the more we hindered our educational and career success, while perpetuating many of the stereotypes associated with our race. It is important that I offer here some strategies for college and university administrators to implement that may aid their Black male populations with circumventing the gangstaism on their campuses.

Because of the racial hostility and social alienation Black males often experience at predominantly White institutions, these colleges and universities should give great consideration to proactive support and intervention strategies to help this population achieve success. Harris, Palmer and Struve (2011) recommended four pre-emptive approaches to reduce the effects of gangsta culture on Black male students. First, institutions should endeavor to establish a stronger Black male presence in their campus support offices (e.g., financial aid, counseling center, student success offices, etc.) to increase the likelihood that Black male students will seek out appropriate assistance when faced with dilemmas of how to adequately express their manhood and cope with various college stressors. Second, these institutions should develop Black male-centered groups that are facilitated by Black male college faculty or staff who understand and have knowledge of challenging issues specific to Black college men, especially on White college campuses. Third, institutions should venture to connect Black college men with older Black males who appropriately express their masculinities such as faculty, staff, recent graduates, or men in the community that can serve as mentors. Lastly, efforts should be made to facilitate professional development opportunities that focus on Black masculinity for faculty and staff who work directly with Black males on campus. Additionally, it may be productive if colleges and universities enlist the assistance of the organizations that these Black males hold in such high regard—the Black Greeks.

Black Greek Fraternities. Black Greek fraternities should also play a major role in Black male students' successful navigation of the gangsta culture on their campuses. These groups should consider organizing orientations (and sessions periodically throughout the school year) for Black freshmen males where they can speak candidly about the pitfalls of college and university life. These orientations should also focus on strategy development for Black males to successfully achieve their manhood and become campus and community leaders without subscribing to the manhood-validating behaviors associated with gangsta culture.

The fraternities could work to incorporate freshmen males in mentoring and other leadership activities early in their college experiences. Greek organizations could conduct regular study workshops to highlight the high regard that the fraternities place on academics and the value they place on the young Black men's success. Fraternities should work harder to do a better job of policing the behaviors of their individual members and the organization as an entity, especially behaviors that contribute to the gangsta culture of their campuses. Campus administration should implement formal success programs that incorporate Black Greek organizations and harness their influence to promote the success of Black males on campuses, academically, emotionally, and socially.

Although these recommendations may not be a panacea for the Black gangstaism on predominantly White college and university campuses, they do provide a basis for action. Building collaborative relationships with the Black Greek fraternities and similar organizations could help the administration in their efforts to combat the gangstaism on their campus. Such efforts could serve as a model for Black leadership in America to work with gangs and gang leaders to deter our young Black men from the perils of the gangsta lifestyle that exists outside of the Ivory tower. If similar structures had been in place when I attended college, I may not have been hindered in my success and many of my friends may have averted falling victim to the campus's Black gangsta culture.

REFERENCES

Collins, P. H. (2004). *Black sexual politics: African Americans, gender, and the new racism.* New York, NY: Routledge.

Cozart, S. C. (2010). When the spirit shows up: An autoethnography of spiritual reconciliation with the academy. *Educational Studies, 46,* 250–269.

Cureton, S. R. (2009). Something wicked this way comes: A historical account of Black gangstaism offers wisdom and warning for African American leadership. *Journal of Black Studies, 40*(2), 347–361.

Du Bois, W. E. B. (1995). *The souls of Black folk.* New York, NY: Penguin Books. (Original work published 1903)

Geto Boys. (1993). Straight gangstaism. On *Til Death Do Us Part* [CD]. Houston, TX: Rap-A-Lot Records.

Harper, S. R. (2004). The measure of a man: conceptualizations of masculinity among high-achieving African American male college students. *Berkeley Journal of Sociology. 48*, 89–107.

Harris, F. III, Palmer, R., & Struve, L. E. (2011). "Cool posing" on campus: A qualitative study of masculinities and gender expression among Black men at a private research institution. *The Journal of Negro Education, 80*(1), (47-62).

Hazell, V., & Clarke, J. (2008). Race and gender in the media: A content analysis of advertisements in two mainstream Black magazines. *Journal of Black Studies, 39*(1), 5–21.

Majors, R., & Mancini-Billson, J. (1992). *Cool pose: The dilemmas of Black manhood in America.* Lexington, MA: Lexington Books.

Oliver, W. (2006). "The streets": An alternative Black male socialization institution. *Journal of Black Studies, 36*(6), 918–937.

Pleck, J. H., & Pleck, E. H. (1980). *The American man.* New York, NY: Prentice-Hall.

Wallace, D. M. (2007). "It's a man thang": Black male gender role socialization and the performance of masculinity in love relationships. *The Journal of Pan African Studies, 1*(7), (11–22).

Contributors

Juanita J. Chinn is a National Institutes of Health Postdoctoral Fellow in the Office of Population Research at Princeton University. She received her Ph.D. in Sociology with a specialization in Demography from the University of Texas at Austin. Her research interests include racial, gender, and socioeconomic disparities in health and mortality in the United States. Some of her published work can be found in *Ethnicity and Disease*, *The Demography of the Hispanic Population*, and *Du Bois Review: Social Research on Race*. She holds an M.A. in Sociology from the University of Texas at Austin and a Sc.B. in Applied Mathematics: Psychology from Brown University.

Stanley K. Ellis currently serves as the Education Director in the College of Medicine curriculum office at the University of Arkansas for Medical Sciences in Little Rock, Arkansas. His current research examines: (1) socialization of Black junior faculty; (2) servant leadership phenomenon among Black faculty; and (3) pre-faculty exposure (PFE) of junior faculty.

Andrea K. Henderson is Assistant Professor of Sociology at the University of South Carolina. She earned her doctoral degree at the University of Texas at Austin. Her research examines the influence of religion on health and family outcomes, with a strong emphasis on the implications of religious institutions, practices, and values among ethnic minorities.

Darryl B. Holloman is Assistant Vice President for Student Affairs–Multicultural Programs at Georgia State University. Dr. Holloman has worked in student and academic affairs for over twenty years. His research examines the progression and persistence of under-represented populations on college campuses.

Darren Kelly currently serves as the chief of staff for Academic Diversity Initiatives (ADI), a portfolio of the Division of Diversity and Community Engagement (DDCE), at The University of Texas at Austin. His previous experience includes three years working in corporate finance and six years as a graduate research assistant and Research and Academic Coordinator with DDCE. A native of Orange County, CA, Dr. Kelly holds a B.S. in Commerce with concentrations in finance and marketing from the University of Virginia, and a M.A. and Ph.D. in sport management from The University of Texas at Austin. Additionally, Dr. Kelly serves as the director of the McNair Scholars Program and assistant director of the African American Male Research Initiative (AAMRI) at the university. He is also active with several local and national organizations. He is married with one son.

LaGarrett King is an Assistant Professor of Secondary Social Studies Education at Clemson University. Dr. King received his B.S. in Social Studies Education from Louisiana State University, M.S. and Ed.S. from Nova Southeastern University, and a doctorate in Curriculum and Instruction (specializing in Social Studies Education) from the University of Texas at Austin. Professor King is a former classroom teacher and has worked for school systems in Texas and Georgia. Dr. King's scholarly focus falls into two interconnected strands of research related to African American history education and Critical Multicultural Education. The first strand examines how schools, teachers, students and the public interpret and pedagogically implement the content of African American history. His second strand focuses on the foundations of curriculum. More specifically, he examines the intellectual and pedagogical history of African Americans' conceptions of Social Studies education. His work has been published in *Multicultural Perspectives, The Social Studies, Theory and Research in Social Education*, and the *Journal of Social Studies Research*. In addition, he has presented at numerous conferences and conducted professional development in local schools and organizations. Dr. King is the recipient of numerous grants, fellowships and awards including the Graduate Student Research Award from the International Society of the Social Studies and the Graduate Continuing Fellowship from the University of Texas at Austin. Dr. King was selected to participate in North Carolina State University's Building Future Faculty Institute in Raleigh, North Carolina.

Dr. Spencer Platt is an Assistant Professor of Higher Education Administration at the University of South Carolina. He earned his doctoral degree from the University of Texas at Austin. His bachelor's degree is from the University of South

Carolina and he holds a M.S. degree from the University of Dayton. His research interests include: Black males in higher education, access to higher education, critical race theory, and the socialization of doctoral students of color at predominantly white universities.

Dr. Richard J. Reddick is an award-winning Associate Professor in Educational Administration, with courtesy appointments in the Department of African and African Diaspora Studies, and the Warfield Center of African and African American Studies. Dr. Reddick is also a fellow with the Division of Diversity and Community Engagement and the Institute for Urban Policy Research and Analysis, all at The University of Texas at Austin. His research focuses on several areas: the experiences of Black faculty and faculty of color at predominantly White institutions; mentoring and developmental relationships between faculty and Black students; and work-life balance in academia. Reddick's research has been published in the *American Educational Research Journal* and *Harvard Educational Review* as well as featured on NPR and the Associated Press, and he has co-authored and co-edited four scholarly volumes. Dr. Reddick holds a master's and doctorate in higher education from Harvard University, and a bachelor's from The University of Texas at Austin. He is married and the father of two children, serves on the boards of two public charter schools, and is actively engaged in organizations focused on improving the quality of life for Black citizens of Austin, Texas.

James Thomas has earned his Bachelor's degrees in English and Mathematics from Concordia University at Austin. He had the privilege of returning to his alma mater to work in the Dean of Students office as Director of Student Activities & Student Government, Director of Intramural Sports and Director of Residential Life. James is pursuing a doctorate in Higher Education Administration.

Patrick E. Turner has over 19 years in higher education working in the areas of budget management, fiscal accountability and academic services. He is an adjunct instructor for the First-Year Experience Program at Georgia State University and also serves as the financial-business manager for the School of Accountancy in the Robinson College of Business. An Alabama native, Dr. Turner received his B.S. in public administration from Kentucky State University, an M.S. in human resource development at Georgia State University and an Ed.D. in Educational Leadership specializing in curriculum and instruction from the University of Phoenix. Dr. Turner's qualitative research explores the challenges and assistors (enablers) millennial freshman students encounter during their first year of college. He serves as a proposal reviewer for the *National Resource Center for The First-Year Experience & Students in Transition* and reviewer for the *Journal of College Student Retention: Research, Theory & Practice*. His research interests focus primarily on the first-year college experience, freshman retention, pedagogy, and curriculum development.

Lemuel W. Watson is Dean of the College of Education at the University of South Carolina, Professor in the Department of Educational Leadership and Policies, and Executive Director for the South Carolina Center for Educational Partnerships. Dr. Watson is the former Executive Director of the Center for P–20 Engagement and Dean of the College of Education at Northern Illinois University; he is also the former Dean for the division of Academic Support at Heartland College. His career spans across various divisions in educational organizations where he has been a teacher, faculty, policy analyst, and administrator. Dr. Watson was a Senior Research Fellow at the C. Houston Center at Clemson University and Research Fellow at the Institute for Southern Studies at University of South Carolina. He is a Fulbright Scholar and has written articles and books, and served as editor for several volumes related to organizational behavior, educational leadership and administration, human development, public policy, K-12 issues, and higher education. He has provided workshops and professional development opportunities to executives, teachers, and administrators in the United States as well as abroad.

ROCHELLE BROCK &
RICHARD GREGGORY JOHNSON III,
Executive Editors

Black Studies and Critical Thinking is an interdisciplinary series which examines the intellectual traditions of and cultural contributions made by people of African descent throughout the world. Whether it is in literature, art, music, science, or academics, these contributions are vast and far-reaching. As we work to stretch the boundaries of knowledge and understanding of issues critical to the Black experience, this series offers a unique opportunity to study the social, economic, and political forces that have shaped the historic experience of Black America, and that continue to determine our future. Black Studies and Critical Thinking is positioned at the forefront of research on the Black experience, and is the source for dynamic, innovative, and creative exploration of the most vital issues facing African Americans. The series invites contributions from all disciplines but is specially suited for cultural studies, anthropology, history, sociology, literature, art, and music.

Subjects of interest include (but are not limited to):

- EDUCATION
- SOCIOLOGY
- HISTORY
- MEDIA/COMMUNICATION
- RELIGION/THEOLOGY
- WOMEN'S STUDIES

- POLICY STUDIES
- ADVERTISING
- AFRICAN AMERICAN STUDIES
- POLITICAL SCIENCE
- LGBT STUDIES

For additional information about this series or for the submission of manuscripts, please contact Dr. Brock (Indiana University Northwest) at brock2@iun.edu or Dr. Johnson (University of San Francisco) at rgjohnsoniii@usfca.edu.

To order other books in this series, please contact our Customer Service Department:

(800) 770-LANG (within the U.S.)
(212) 647-7706 (outside the U.S.)
(212) 647-7707 FAX

Or browse online by series at www.peterlang.com.

www.ingramcontent.com/pod-product-compliance
Ingram Content Group UK Ltd.
Pitfield, Milton Keynes, MK11 3LW, UK
UKHW022239230426
12048UKWH00018BA/1359